COMBAT
SELLING

COMBAT SELLING

Battle Strategies for Sales Leaders

DALE MILLAR

*A leader's guide to using the fundamental principles
of war as a framework for vision, strategy, planning,
and successful sales execution.*

Published by Wheatmark®
1760 East River Road, Suite 145
Tucson, Arizona 85718 USA
www.wheatmark.com

ISBN: 978-1-62787-077-1 (paperback)
ISBN: 978-1-62787-078-8 (ebook)
LCCN: 2013953762

To Dad
22/12/1931 – 10/11/2013

Contents

Foreword

As chairman and CEO of ThruPoint, Inc., an international software and professional services house based in New York City, I have no doubt about the fundamental importance of sales to a business. Without an effectively led, organized, motivated, and delivering sales force, a company simply cannot succeed.

Here at ThruPoint, I put tremendous emphasis on selling in my daily schedule. And while product development, marketing, administration, finance, and human resources take up much of my attention, I never lose my focus on "the number," "the pipeline," and "the commit."

I've known Dale Millar for a number of years and have found him to be an innovative and successful salesperson. But what interests me most about him is the way he has taken his sales effectiveness to new levels. He has developed a thoughtful and impactful approach to sales leadership—the key theme of this book.

I've seen many failing sales teams over the years that may lack spirit, product knowledge, closing skills, or thorough organization. In every case, they share a common theme—poor leadership. While it may be an exaggeration to say there are no poor salespeople, only poor sales managers, it's undeniable that the way sales teams are led is critical to their success.

Combat Selling provides a structured, comprehensive approach to the sales leadership process. The concept of utilizing the military's principles of war as a framework for the text is both interesting and enlightening. It reflects the highly competitive and combative nature of today's global markets. I found myself continually astonished at the parallels to historical military engagements and my experiences with sales teams fighting to win business against aggressive competitors. I believe all readers will be able to reflect and benefit in the same way I did.

At ThruPoint, we're dedicated to excellence in everything we do, and I put a lot of emphasis on planning accounts and setting objectives. Dale's ideas on how to structure these processes provide guidance and rigor, while his approaches to maintaining momentum—through aggressive spirit, the need to keep saying yes, the concentration of resources, and the reinforcement of success—are all critical tenets of our success.

I particularly enjoyed *Combat Selling*'s take on competitive readiness and the need to ensure sales teams are properly prepared to go into the market. I see too many ill-prepared salespeople in my office to ignore the need to have a punctilious attitude toward preparation and planning.

Finally, regarding the conduct of campaigns, we've all experienced the pain of defeat in a hard-fought competition for a particular piece of business. It's not a result any of us enjoys. While *Combat Selling*'s advice on campaign conduct won't guarantee you'll never lose another deal, it does mean you will *win* more business through better organization, flexibility, and optimum utilization of your resources.

Dale has produced an exciting, powerful, and intensely practical book on sales leadership. It will give you a new perspective on how to manage your sales teams and win more business in an ever more competitive marketplace.

I have no hesitation in recommending it to you as an enjoyable, informative, and ultimately business-enhancing guide.

Great selling!

Rami Musallam, Chairman and CEO, ThruPoint, Inc.

New York City, April 2013

Introduction

What's This Book About?

Selling is the most important part of any business—bar none. Of course, great products, top quality, and sound finances are critical components of the mix. But without an effective sales force and a robust go-to-market strategy, it's all for naught.

Having been in sales for more than twenty years, I came to realize the criticality of what I was doing was similar to the huge responsibility one carries when serving in the military, which I'd done for the previous ten years. Not only that, but the rigors of the sales effort—with its moments of unbearably high tension, ups and downs in fortune, intense pressure to succeed, and unpredictable behavior of the customer—make it analogous to combat.

I've also noted that the type of people who succeed in sales have a lot in common with high-quality soldiers. They're courageous and full of initiative and self-belief. They're able to persevere under difficult circumstances. They're possessed of a strong sense of urgency and a refuse-to-lose attitude in the face of enemy or competitive pressure.

That being true, I've taken some of the practical principles, techniques, and methodologies the military teaches officers and applied them to sales leadership. In addition, I've included all of the effective solutions and approaches to sales management I've used during my business career. Thus, this book, *Combat Selling*, is a how-to guide for those interested in leading sales teams and achieving high-performance results.

Who Is It For?

Combat Selling is for business people who need to understand the mechanics of sales leadership and want to formalize this skill (often regarded as a "black art") using a structured and scientific framework. However, though military principles are being used as a foundation because they're remarkably well suited to the selling environment, you needn't be an ex-soldier or a budding combatant to benefit.

As a reader, you've probably come from a corporation, a midmarket company, or a small/medium enterprise (SME). The principles and techniques apply to selling across the board; it's merely a matter of adapting them for scale.

You'll see many of my real life examples come from the high-technology segment, but that's because they reflect my experiences; it's not meant to limit this book's content to Silicon Valley leaders only.

In short, if you want to run a successful sales team, this book is for you.

Why the Military Angle?

The militaries of the United States, United Kingdom, and Russia have established sets of principles that provide an overall framework for the conduct of their operations. To be clear, I would never want to denigrate the amazing work done by our soldiers, marines, sailors, and airmen by comparing their brave, selfless sacrifices with the less frantic and clearly less dangerous world of selling.

I do strongly believe, however, that business people can learn a huge amount by applying certain military principles to the sales environment. Here's an overview of what I mean:

- **Operational and campaign planning**—Military leaders formulate and execute different plans every day. Their sales teams need to adopt a similarly disciplined approach to the planning process.

- **Selection and maintenance of objectives**—Taking the plan and creating a set of objectives all the way down to the individual soldier or salesperson is critical to successful execution.

- **Offensive action**—Getting your unit or team to adopt an aggressive and offensive spirit is key to success in both battle and business.

- **Concentration of resources**—For the military, maximizing force at the enemy's weak point is a sure way to gain strategic advantage. In business, ensuring you concentrate your sales resources on the most lucrative and well-qualified customers and deals is an effective way to generate sales.

- **High combat readiness**—To be successful in battle, troops need to be trained, motivated, and equipped. To do battle in business, sales teams need to be properly briefed, equipped with the right materials, and highly incentivized to succeed.

- **Leadership and the maintenance of morale**—Military history is replete with examples of how high morale and esprit de corps can be leveraged to win battles more effectively than force of numbers or tactical advantage. In business, teams that are well led and maintain a high level of morale infect their customers with the same strong, positive attitude toward the company and its products. These qualities lead to better sales.

- **Unity of command**—War requires a clear chain of command and individual leaders who have ultimate authority to execute the mission. In sales, the modern trend toward matrix management leads to lack of clarity, loss of momentum, and confusion for the customer. This book demonstrates the advantages of executing a mission the military way.

- **Economy of force**—In both war and business, making sure that every individual is totally consumed with achieving the common goal is the *only* way to fulfill the modern demands of doing more with less.

- **Maneuvers**—Battles are often won by a general outmaneuvering his foe, thereby catching him by surprise and off balance. Successful sales campaigns often require strategic changes in direction and maneuvering of customer requirements to put competition at a disadvantage.

- **Security**—Keeping your intentions secret from the enemy is a fundamental underpinning of military operations. Information security and the flip side—knowledge of competition—are often critical factors in successful sales campaigns.

- **Flexibility**—Flexible approaches win battles and business. You instinctively know that stick-in-the-mud attitudes upset customers and colleagues, but for some reason, those attitudes are hard to prevent.

- **Perseverance**—Persisting in the face of seemingly insurmountable difficulties characterizes both soldiers and successful salespeople.

- **Simplicity**—The maxim "Keep it simple, stupid" is at home both on the battlefield and in the office. Complexity makes it difficult for everyone to understand the mission and its execution. When things go wrong, initiative is suppressed by confusion.

- **Legitimacy**—Conducting one's business in an illegitimate fashion has undermined whole corporations and thousands of promising careers in recent years. The need to enunciate, understand, and obey rules in business has never been greater than it is today. Just as soldiers have to obey the basic codes of combat, business people need to be clearly above reproach in the way they conduct themselves.

I hope you'll be inspired to apply several of these principles to the framework of your own leadership approach and employ the techniques with your own teams. I sincerely believe you'll find *Combat Selling* to be entertaining, interesting, and ultimately profitable.

And now—into battle!

1 Planning for Sales

In preparing for battle I have always found that plans are useless, but planning is indispensable.—**Dwight D. Eisenhower**, *US president*

The method of the enterprising is to plan with audacity and execute with vigor.—**Christian Nestell Bovee**, *American writer*

Introduction

The militaries of the world all have a principle of war based on the concept of operational art and campaign planning. It's fundamental to the way they go about their business. With that in mind, I'm addressing the need for careful planning in the sales process—and the fundamental role planning plays in the overall success of the sales effort—right at the start. As the discussion about the overall art of sales unfolds, I continually mention the need to have all members of the sales team working in a coordinated, focused, and concentrated fashion on key target areas. However, unless you properly follow the planning process and produce an excellent, achievable, and flexible plan, such coordination and focus are difficult, if not impossible, to achieve.

Military units are good at planning. They need to be. They have a multitude of differing resources and an intensely adverse and unpredictable environment in which to operate. They often face tenuous communications and an enemy whose sole intention is to throw as many wrenches in the works as possible.

Given the world's armed forces' history of successes, it's entirely reasonable to use a military framework to structure our sales planning process. Because this typically produces a good plan, it provides us with

One can only regard with awe and wonder the astonishing achievements of General Eisenhower's staff in 1944. The staff put together the logistical and operational plans that allowed 130,000 troops, 300 battle ships, 270 minesweepers, and hundreds of aircraft and gliders to invade France on D-Day—dubbed Operation Overlord. The invasion utilized the forces of a dozen countries, was coordinated with the Resistance in France, and even ran a complex deception plan to fool the Germans into thinking the landings were going to take place elsewhere. All of this planning was achieved in the first six months of 1944 without computers, Internet, or video through the use of typewriters, messengers, and rudimentary (and quite insecure) telephone systems. Such a feat makes even the most complex parts of the jobs most of us do nowadays seem remarkably straightforward.

a solid foundation on which to build strategies that the principles of warfare bring to our selling effort.

Specifically, the British army uses an overview of campaigning, which creates an ideal framework to discuss the sales planning process—from initial concept through vision, plan creation, and plan execution. The five key areas of the model include the following:

- **Operational command**—the central tenet around which the entire operation runs

- **Operational art**—the identification of what will be decisive beforehand and the shaping of the operation for success

- **Operational design**—the commander's vision of how the operation will unfold

- **Campaign planning**—the detail of the campaign

- **Operational management**—how the campaign is managed and executed doesn't provide a way to measure success or contribute to the planning process.

Instead, create something with teeth, like this:

> We aim to achieve market leadership for our enhanced software suite in commercial and retail banking in all major countries of EMEA* and the United States/Canada within a four-year period. Sales operations must focus on closing deals with three of the top five players in each geographical region.

Everyone can rally around a powerful statement like this. This example of a succinct vision states what's required, making it easy to write a strategy. Some companies put their vision statements on plastic the size of a credit card and encourage staff members to attach it to their ID badges. It sends this message to staff members: "If you're about to do something that isn't related to achieving this vision, it's probably best you don't do it."

An effective vision statement has a time horizon of three to five years. It needs to be ambitious and also provide everything the stakeholders in the company would expect over that period in terms of profit, share price, dividends, and the like.

Sales Strategy (Two- to Three-Year Horizon)

Operational design, the military equivalent of sales strategy, is a way of refining and developing the static vision into a "video," if you will, of how the commander sees the operation unfolding. In a sales context, sales strategy identifies the key threads of the sales leader's approach that will enable planners to implement the vision in the best way.

Going forward, I'll use the hypothetical example of BankSoft, the software company with the previously presented vision statement. BankSoft is forming a division to focus on a new product suite specifically developed for the banking sector. This simplified model illustrates a clear framework of the vision-strategy-planning process.

---

* Europe, the Middle East, and Africa

The company's strategy includes the following seven critical strategic thrusts:

- **Deployment**—Establish sales and presales teams in central hubs for each major geography.

- **Support**—Provide post-sales customer service from "follow-the-sun" locations (referring to teams dispersed around the globe so there are always people working in daylight hours providing 24/7 coverage), with scalability to support up to two hundred major customers.

- **Product**—Create development teams to tailor the product for specific customers.

- **Pricing**—Develop a flexible licensing and pricing model to suit the needs of large banking customers.

- **Marketing**—Focus all marketing efforts on large players, and target accordingly.

- **Competition**—Keep a sharp focus on competition from AcmeSoft and other emerging players in terms of differentiation, functionality, and value.

- **Talent**—Build a cohort of talented sales, engineering, and marketing professionals on which to base success.

The strategy then provides an execution overlay (see table 1.1). This further level of detail allows for the creation of a specific location or geography-level plan.

The strategy then provides an execution overlay (see table 1.1). This further level of detail allows for the creation of a specific location or geography-level plan.

Table 1.1
BankSoft's Sales Strategy Execution Overlay for Its New Software Division

Strategic Thrust	Execution
Deployment	Deploy regional teams to: • Frankfurt • London • Dubai • Johannesburg • New York • Los Angeles • Toronto
	Hire or determine a sales director based in London and one in New York to run the EMEA and US/Canada geographies respectively. 　　Hire or determine the regional teams, which consist of: • Regional sales manager • Account managers x 4 • Presales engineers x 5 • Sales operations executor x 1 • Administrator x 1
Support	Prepare customer-service centers in Sioux City, Iowa, and Bangalore, India, in such a way that the centers can expand to support new customers as they are won. This will involve continual overmanning to track ahead of the sales forecast.
Product	Complete banking software suite ready to ship by start of the financial year (FY).
	Properly staff development teams to cope with specific modifications for individual customers.
	Recruit partner organization to provide complementary applications to support additional customer requirements.
	Set up infrastructure to prioritize and rationalize product modifications that will prevent duplication and minimize delay.

Strategic Thrust	Execution
Pricing	Create global price list.
	Create discounting authorization solution to ensure the sales teams have controlled flexibility on pricing.
	Create mechanism that allows rapid pricing of modifications and accurate timelines for implementation.
Marketing	Create a team of five marketing personnel to address online, print, and exhibition marketing effort.
	Develop marketing plan to address all markets; carefully link it to the sales forecast.
	Ensure sufficient budget to support the sales forecast.
Competition	Create a plan to defeat AcmeSoft in every market.
	Analyze the AcmeSoft pricing model and ensure that our sales teams can demonstrate superior value for money by creating value-based comparisons.
	Provide sales teams with ongoing guidance about what AcmeSoft personnel are saying about us and about AcmeSoft, and provide contrary view and rebuttals when necessary.
Talent	Build and execute a plan through human resources to recruit top talent in every market for sales and presales activity.
	Make a specific effort to retain new and existing talent and to recycle underperformers.

Before the detailed planning process can begin, the company needs to disseminate target numbers and budgets. Don't provide only raw revenue, profit, and overhead numbers. Ensure that product mix is added to the plan; failure to do this could lead to unbalanced sales across the portfolio.

By now, you can see how the leader's vision flows down through the process from vision through strategy to an executable plan.

At this point, the company develops a table specifying key numbers allocated across the portfolio, as illustrated in table 1.2.

Table 1.2
BankSoft's Key Numbers Allocated Across Its Portfolio

Geography	Product	Turnover (M$)	Margin (M$)	Overhead (M$)	Unloaded EBITDA (Earnings Before Interest, Tax, and Depreciation) (M$)
Frankfurt	Assets	$20.00	$14.00		
	Liabilities	$26.00	$18.00		
	Credit Card System	$35.00	$25.00		
	Total	$81.00	$57.00	$42.00	$15.00
London	Assets	$18.00	$12.00		
	Liabilities	$24.00	$17.00		
	Credit Card System	$33.00	$24.00		
	Total	$75.00	$53.00	$42.00	$11.00
	Etc.				

Sales Plan

As it puts together its detailed plans, the military uses a number of concepts that provide useful guidelines for sales leaders. The following five concepts translate across the military-civilian divide:

- **Centers of gravity**—key capabilities of both your company and the competition

- **End-state modeling**—where the company wants to be at the end of the planned window

- **Decisive points**—often referred to as "must wins"

- **Sequencing and phases**—ordering what needs to be done to achieve a victory at the decisive point

- **Contingency planning**—what to do if (and/or when) things don't go according to plan

---

In the Yom Kippur War of 1973, the Egyptian invasion force's Third Army was definitely the center of gravity of the offensive. The formation had crossed the Suez Canal into Sinai and was at the vanguard of the attack. The Israeli Defense Force identified the criticality of the Third Army and was able to undermine the entire Egyptian war effort. General Ariel Sharon's 143rd Division launched a successful counterattack at Chinese Farm, which eventually led to the encirclement and defeat of the Third Army. With the COG destroyed, the Egyptians were forced onto the defensive. The war ended with Israeli tanks only one hundred kilometers from Cairo.

In this case, the Egyptians had a critical vulnerability in a gap between the Second and Third Armies that allowed the Israelis to make a lightly opposed counterattack over the Suez Canal. The Israelis had identified and attacked the Egyptians' COG and its vulnerability with extreme vigor.

Following is a detailed discussion of these concepts to show what you can gain from using them in your own selling environment.

Centers of gravity (COG): Both you and your competition have centers of gravity. I define these as elements of the business that would fatally flaw your overall sales effort if undermined. You need to define your COGs and defend them with vigor. Also identify your competitors' COGs so you can attack them with intensity.

An excellent business example of how this works is illustrated by Chinese telecommunications manufacturers such as Huawei and ZTE, which are addressing the home markets of the established Western players such as Ericsson, Alcatel-Lucent, and Nokia Siemens Networks. The Chinese companies know these Western players have COGs comprised of large installed bases of equipment with the major telcos in the West and that their key vulnerability is their high pricing (based on their high cost base). The Chinese have successfully attacked these COGs with what appears to be suicidal low pricing, advantageous terms and conditions, and support contracts their Western competition can't possibly match. The result? Not only have the Chinese achieved significant market penetration, but the undermining of their competitors' COGs is, in some cases, having a disastrous effect on the competition's viability.

It's critical to make a conscious effort in the planning process to look for COGs on both sides of the fence. Once they've been identified, make sure you put defensive plans in place to protect your own COG and find ways to attack the COGs of the competition.

End-state modeling: End-state modeling should be much easier in business than in the military. You'd think it would be relatively easy from the sales vision and sales strategy to figure out exactly what's required from the execution plan and how it will be measured. But you'd be astonished at the number of salespeople who have no idea what to do *and* what end state they're trying to achieve. Most of them know what their target number is, but often that's it.

End-state modeling shouldn't be limited to accounts and deals to capture; it also needs to consider the environmental conditions required to sustain the desired end point. What will the support infrastructure look like to provide excellent customer service? What type of account management teams will be required to maintain newly won accounts?

Will the people who won the account be the right ones to sustain it—
and if not, where will you get people who can fill the role?

In recent years, the military has struggled much more with end-state modeling
than in the past. For example, at the end of the first Gulf War in 1990, despite the
success of the US Army's AirLand Battle doctrine in routing the Iraqi Army from
Kuwait, Iraq remained a threat to US interests in the region, and the Iraqi president
remained in place. This was not at all expected.

Indeed, the United States had to invade Iraq in 2003 to force a regime
change at enormous human and financial cost. It appears the United States gave
little thought to the idea of regime change after the second Gulf War ended two
months later. Having disbanded the Ba'ath party and its infrastructure, the Allies
essentially left the country open to chaos.

In both the first and second Gulf Wars, one has to question whether end-
state planning was properly considered. Had a postwar end state been carefully
modeled, the outcome may have been much better. In the case of the first Gulf
War, a successful ceasefire and peace settlement may well have averted the need
for a second war.

Decisive points (DPs): Often referred to as "must wins" in sales,
DPs are typically accounts or deals that have to be won for the overall
plan to be successful. Most sales plans include some decisive points that
have to be addressed and closed at all costs.

The key is for business to identify their decisive points and then
direct maximum resources at them. Identifying target DPs is crucial so
everyone understands their significance and acts accordingly.

Sequencing and phases: The armed forces use a framework called
the military decision-making process model (MDMP) that endeavors to
execute a parallel planning process for concurrent activity with a flow
of instructions from top to bottom. In the civilian context, this process
is often impaired; instructions aren't passed down in a timely manner,
so people at the base of the command structure often get short notice
of fresh orders. Because they have little chance to prepare, execution is
impeded.

In the military, the commander receives instructions from a higher authority and then conducts a process of analyzing and planning before issuing a more detailed set of instructions to subordinate organizations. These subordinate commanders, in turn, analyze and produce instructions to pass down the line. The military ethos encourages parallel planning and concurrent activity at all levels. Commanders are trained to send warning orders to subordinate formations to ensure they're making preparations even though they don't yet have a full set of instructions. Preparing may mean striking camp, collecting ammunition, refueling, feeding, or undergoing special mission rehearsals. An excellent rule the military adopted is the law of thirds, which advocates using one-third of the total time available to plan and passing two-thirds of the time to your subordinates. The subordinates do the same and pass two-thirds of the time they've been given down the line to the next level.

Everyone needs time to prepare for activity, and while it's acknowledged that the commander needs the most time, monopolizing it gives no opportunity for subordinates to prepare to succeed.

The same thing applies in business. Many sales teams complain of persistent "fire drills" and "diving catches" as crises seem to wash over them with alarming regularity. As a sales leader, you want to avoid this to prevent a staccato approach to selling. Make sure that at the first sign of a problem or new requirement information is passed to the teams so they can prepare. This may be anything from a product recall or a lengthening of delivery times to an account in transition. In a world where teams are often geographically dispersed, it's important to over-communicate your plans so you get adequate warning of upcoming events that can disrupt them.

Contingency planning: Businesses can learn a lot from military contingency planning. By the nature of military operations, people are frequently taken out of action, but this can never be allowed to foil the mission. The same applies to units that become noncombat effective because of enemy action or logistical failures. In all cases, contingency plans are made so individuals can take over command and units can act as reinforcements. These contingencies are planned and rehearsed—a completely normal part of the military process.

Similarly, in business there's a need to be able to carry out any particular plan if a key individual becomes sick or leaves. This means the division needs to develop a written and well-publicized succession plan. In addition, individuals are required to take responsibility for ensuring their designates are well briefed and updated on the current state of the business.

From a customer perspective, sales teams require a backup in terms of deals that could be closed or customers who could be acquired with the application of more resources. This is true especially when deals in the pipeline could be disqualified. (I will say more on this when discussing forecasts and pipelines.) Be aware that early warning of deals going south is critical so valuable time and effort isn't wasted on dying deals. As an excellent sales director I knew in the United States would say, "If you're going to lose a deal, lose it early." By this, he meant it's better to get out of a losing deal before you commit a large amount of time and resources to it.

At this point, the contingency plan comes into its own. It will include a number of new customers and deals that may not have been decisive points at the start, but given the loss of other deals, may get elevated in status. This means diverting teams away from the failing or lost deal and realistically addressing new ones.

Planning Process

By way of example, let's continue the banking software scenario and look at BankSoft's planning process in Frankfurt.

Let's assume BankSoft's financial and calendar years coincide and the sales vision, sales strategy, and execution come to the regional manager in Frankfurt at the start of November. The manager's director has known the wider picture since the start of October and has used one-third of the time to build the plan for the whole of EMEA. The regional manager now has three weeks to make plans for the account managers before giving them five weeks before year-end to make plans for the following period. It's the rule of thirds in action.

Table 1.3

Planning Time According to the Rule of Thirds

Level	Oct.	Nov.	Dec.	Potential Days Available	Days Used	Days Passed Down
Sales Director	▓▓▓			90	30	60
Regional Manager		▓▓		60	20	40
Account Manager			▓▓▓	40	40	–

The plan coming down the line gives the Frankfurt team these numbers:

Table 1.4

Plan Numbers for the Frankfurt Team

Geography	Product	Turn-over (M$)	Margin (M$)	Over-head (M$)	Un-loaded EBITDA (M$)
	Assets	$ 20.00	$ 14.00		
	Liabilities	$ 26.00	$ 18.00		
Frankfurt	Credit Card System	$ 35.00	$ 25.00		
	Total	$ 81.00	$ 57.00	$ 42.00	$ 15.00

The team members have also been told to focus on the top three to five banks in their geography with the new banking software suite. Remember, this direction comes from the sales vision. The director will probably have named the accounts of interest in his briefing, but in this case, the sales manager is tasked with allocating numbers to accounts.

Next comes extraction of orders—the process of taking the high-level instructions and applying them to the lower-level organization. The execution piece would extract for the Frankfurt team as follows:

Table 1.5
Execution for the Frankfurt Team

Strategic Thrust	Execution
Deployment	The Frankfurt regional team is to include: • Regional sales manager • Account managers x 4 • Presales engineers x 5 • Sales operations executor x 1 • Administrator x 1 (The sales manager realizes he needs to expand his team to fit this manpower profile.)
Support	Frankfurt's customers will be supported from Bangalore for the first half of the day and from Sioux City for the second.
Product	Complete banking software suite will be ready to ship by the start of FY. All modules to customers will be pitched immediately.
	Properly staff the development teams to cope with specific modifications for individual customers. German, Austrian, and Swiss customers are notoriously demanding, so the team needs to be prepared to pitch tailored specifications to meet their needs.
	Recruit a partner organization to provide complementary applications to support additional customer requirements. The sales manager will work with the corporate channel organization to bring in local partners quickly.

Strategic Thrust	Execution
Pricing	Make available a global price list for immediate quotation preparation.
	Train sales teams on the new discount-approval system.
	Ensure the sales teams understand product modification tools to provide customers with accurate costs and delivery timings.
Marketing	Provide local marketing from a central team.
	Have the Frankfurt team liaise with the central team to build a local marketing plan.
	Ensure the Frankfurt team understands how to bid for resources.
Competition	Identify AcmeSoft as the key competitor.
	Look for AcmeSoft's center of gravity and attack its decisive points.
	Ensure that the central team provides all competitive information and tool sets.
Talent	Ensure that the recruiting and retention of the team is properly executed.
	Recycle underperformers.

At this point, the sales manager in Frankfurt has gained clarity about what's expected of him. He knows the accounts he has to target and the products he needs to sell. He knows how those products will be supported, what personnel budget he has, if he has to recruit or not, who his main competitor is, and therefore what he needs to target—a lot of highly specific information. Similarly, sales organizations can learn from this military model when compiling high-level vision, strategy, and execution information and directing it down to the lowest levels of the organization.

Execution Overlay

The Frankfurt sales manager can write his plan, which will form the basis for his entire year. He'll use it to brief the entire Frankfurt team on the overall approach and drive individual objectives and number targets for the salespeople. He can allocate accounts, and every individual on the team will clearly be told what's required.

Sales Targets

For the team to be successful, who has to get which numbers? Leaders must consider the following factors:

- **The propensity of the customer to take certain volumes and types of product**—Before you write the plan, find out the customer's procurement intentions, current purchasing preferences, and budget availability. Does the customer have an immediate requirement, or will you have to create demand? Will you need to dislodge an incumbent provider?

- **The length of the sales cycle with any given product**— Some products (particularly hardware) have relatively rapid sales cycles due to customer expansion or upgrading of products. Software solutions can be slow to move depending on the circumstances. However, extra licenses, complementary applications, Web-based upgrades, and so forth can speed things up, so there's no one-size-fits-all approach. Find out the customers' needs.

- **The level of difficulty of working with particular customers**—Some customers are slow to make decisions, highly demanding of you and your team, procurement driven, unresponsive despite being resource intensive, and often downright obstreperous.

After having analyzed what you can expect from individual customers, I recommend using the following matrix as a guide to building the sales numbers.

Table 1.6
Matrix for Building Sales Numbers

Account Manager	Account	Assets (M$)	Liabilities (M$)	Credit Card System (M$)	Total (M$)
AM #1	Bank A	$ 2.00	$ 4.00	$ 4.00	**$ 10.00**
	Bank B	$ 3.00	$ 2.50	$ 5.00	**$ 10.50**
	Total	$5.00	$ 6.50	$ 9.00	$ 20.50
AM #2	Bank C	$ 2.00	$ 3.50	$ 3.00	**$ 8.50**
	Bank D	$ 2.00	$ 2.50	$ 5.00	**$ 9.50**
	Total	$4.00	$ 6.00	$ 8.00	$ 18.00
Etc.					

In most cases, distributing margin targets is not necessary because pricing will be controlled and approved within your organization. The salespeople will be given price negotiation windows, and these control the requisite margin.

Planning Concepts

Let's continue our example of the Frankfurt SoftBank team.

What About "Over-Goaling"?

I'm often asked about my opinion on "over-goaling"—the practice of giving account managers a bigger goal than necessary to achieve the overall regional number. This does provide contingencies if things aren't working out. At least some of the account managers will be on target, and you can use this to backfill any underperformance in other accounts. That said, I don't think it's good practice and here's why:

- I prefer openness with teams. It's much better to fully understand the actual challenge for the group and address it together than to try to manipulate it.
- If everyone up the chain of command attempts to "over-goal," then the number that finally lands in the inbox of the poor account manager is unrealistically overloaded.
- The propensity for getting pay plans confused is great. I like to keep things as simple as possible in an environment that's already complex.

- **Our center of gravity**—In the case of the Frankfurt operation, essentially a start-up, the COG will come from good relationships in four of the targeted eight banks at the level of CxO—meaning a top C-suite executive (i.e., CIO, CMO, CEO)—as well as from an installed base of software in the region and an excellent track record for service. Finally, we have a vibrant new team with good funding and a strong plan.

- **Competition center of gravity**—AcmeSoft has an installed base in six of the eight targeted banks and an active team working the Frankfurt area. The situation presents a daunting challenge.

- **End state**—The goal is to achieve penetration in all targeted banks based on the sales numbers. This means displacing AcmeSoft in at least some of the operations in all of the banks.

- **Our decisive points**—AcmeSoft will attack us on the basis of the newness of our products and our lack of installed base.

- **Competition decisive points**—In at least one operation in each of the targeted banks, AcmeSoft is doing a bad job. Customers are unhappy with its out-of-date functionality, low levels of timely support, and high cost of modifications. In addition, a lack of competition has made the sales force arrogant and difficult to deal with. It appears that AcmeSoft is ripe for the taking.

- **Contingency planning**—Although we've targeted eight banks, we need to build a pipeline with a secondary tier of four banks, one per account manager, which will be a contingency against failure at the primary targets. However, this can't use up an inordinate amount of resources. At the same time, we need to address the second tier adequately.

Loose ends such as marketing, recruitment, training, and talent management remain; these can be addressed locally depending on company resources and culture.

At this point, it's time to build your forecast—the focal point of every sales effort. But first let's look at the critical role of sales management in the overall planning activity.

Sales Management

Like its counterpart in the military, sales management in business runs at many levels. The first-line manager and his account managers constitute a key unit forming the base of a pyramid that has several layers. At its apex is a sales vice president, who controls multiple geographies or segments. At all levels, the company's sales leaders will need to build a capability to control the teams and drive performance.

At the lowest level, the sales manager will have around six account managers, and control is relatively informal. The manager will be calling direct reports and their support teams every day and will probably spend a day every two weeks with each of them in the field. Today, many managers have the advantage of real-time business information systems online, although many still use spreadsheets (or the back of cigarette packages) to assemble numbers and customer data while talking over the phone.

In any event, at this level, good first-line managers will be in complete control of what their people are doing and how well they're doing it, what the performance is in terms of numbers, and what will be booking in the coming days and weeks.

For salespeople needing to be busy all the time, tempo and rhythm are critical concepts. The best way to drive useful activity is to be out calling on customers.

A good salesperson is continually on the phone talking to and making new contacts, building a story through a continual process of discovery, and working out how to penetrate at multiple points in the organization. He or she wants to know what can be done to help the customer address current issues. Over the course of a few weeks, a good salesperson aims to build a warm rapport.

The sales manager is critical in driving the tempo of her team. To ensure their people are highly active, sales managers may check diaries, phone logs, and visit reports. They look for growth in the pipeline and a continual shift from speculative to fully committed opportunities. Most of all, they lead by example with constant, highly charged activity every day and don't micromanage unless necessary.

The work of the second-level sales manager (often referred to as the sales director) is more abstract and comes with a reliance on business-information systems to monitor performance. In addition, the forecast becomes a key tool in analyzing progress and deciding changes in direction. Although high-quality data is critical, it's not wise to allow second-line managers and their teams to become pure desk jockeys, monitoring what the troops are doing and not making a material difference to the overall effort. These second-line managers should be holding weekly review meetings and spending time in the field with first-line managers. Otherwise, they can't effectively run the sales-management organizations.

At the vice-president (VP) level, feeling isolated from the sales effort is difficult to prevent. VPs depend on business information and regular reviews to establish the teams' level of performance. In effect, a good VP visits customers every week, but mainly matches the sales vision and strategy with what's unfolding on the ground, and then takes corrective actions to keep the teams on course.

The Forecast

What's the single-most important part of the sales team's reporting and command structure? The forecast. Absolutely pivotal to all sales activities, it needs to be accurate and realistic as well as carefully monitored for growth, improvement, and veracity. To do this well takes skill, discipline, and persistence.

Every salesperson needs to identify the deals he or she will be doing in the forecast period. Therefore, paying attention to the following information is critical:

- **Customer name and department/subsidiary**—It's important to nail down which part of a business you're engaging because many customers are comprised of clusters of companies that may be only loosely connected. Thus, failure to specify which part of the business you're targeting can lead to confusion.

- **Products and services**—It's excellent discipline to specify early the exact nature of what you're selling, even though this may change greatly over the evolution of the deal. Specificity forces the team to ask the right questions and the customer to think seriously about what's needed.

- **Revenue amount**—Of course, including projected revenue is critical to the forecast.

- **Booking date**—This crucial date triggers the revenue profile for any particular period. It allows the leadership team to understand where it's likely to stand compared to its target at any given time. Unfortunately (but sometimes necessary) for the salespeople, it also provides leaders with prompts for when to chase their salespeople to book more business.

- **Margin**—If salespeople request special discounts, these need to be flagged and approved or declined.

- **Additional resources required**—The salespeople have to identify what, if any, specialist presales personnel they'll require and when they're likely to engage them. In addition, if product modification will be required, salespeople have to indicate this at an early stage.

- **Forecast state**—The idea is to let the leadership team know the likelihood of a particular deal, which is more subjective than some of the other information. The forecast state also provides the company with a pipeline of deals expected to close in the period.

Three-Stage Forecast-State Model

Many companies use a **probability of success** percentage for every deal. However, I find this torturous because teams often argue about whether a deal is 65 percent or 60 percent likely to close, which is pointless. I prefer a three-stage forecast-state model as follows:

- **Commit**—This deal is certain to happen at the time forecast. The sales team has qualified it, the customer has bought in, and the team is addressing all impediments to success. All teams need to understand that when they commit a deal it's a serious matter because everyone expects it to happen. If it doesn't, that becomes a big issue. At the same time, if the system is too draconian, no one will ever commit anything, so balance is needed.
- **Upside**—This deal is certainly looking like it will happen, but significant qualifying steps are still required before it can be a commit. In the meantime, the team has planned significant activity and arranged to make it happen.
- **Prospect**—This is still only a prospective deal. The team has engaged the customer but is still solidifying the requirements. More qualification is required before the deal becomes an upside piece of business.

This forecast state is important because teams build a pipeline of deals that are at various points in the sales cycle. Most deals will enter the forecasts as prospects and work their way through to commits before closing, if all goes well.

Obviously, deals will drop out of all categories, but it's better to see them disappear from the prospect than the commit stage. As a sales leader, be sure to encourage aggressive forecasting and getting as many deals—and as much information—into the forecast as possible. This takes thorough empathy with the salespeople. Strongly warn them not to sandbag—the ancient salesperson's art of keeping a deal secret and then suddenly dropping it into the forecast just before it closes. That can lead to pressuring to bring it in. Sandbagging is not only unprofessional but also robs the company of the chance to:

- up sell through additional presale resource allocation,

- adequately plan for manufacture, and

- supply the stock market with accurate long-term information that could boost share price.

This particular problem perpetuates this undesirable behavior. At the grueling end of a period push to close deals, managers openly welcome an unexpected "blue bird" deal that fills a gap. They're only human, after all. By all means, they should book it, but they also need to hold the salesperson accountable to understand how the deal could have come from out of the blue.

The length of the forecast period depends on the company's sales cycle. I suggest a minimum of two quarters and maximum of four quarters, unless you're working on massive capital projects. In that case, sales cycles last for years.

The Pipeline

Once the forecast is built, it's possible to see a pipeline of deals emerging. The pipeline will likely contain a mix of commits, upsides, and prospects. These are distributed across a timeline, thus indicating to the manager and everyone else the nature of the potential bookings over the course of the period.

Table 1.7a

Pipeline at Start of Q1
$ Millions

	Q1	Q2	Q3	Q4
Commit	1	2	2	3
Upside	2	4	6	8
Prospect	4	7	10	12

Table 1.7b

Pipeline at Start of Q2
$ Millions

	Q1 (Actuals)	Q2	Q3	Q4
Commit	5	4	6	5
Upside		5	8	10
Prospect		4	12	14

Table 1.7c
Pipeline Evolution
$ Millions

	Q1	Q2
Annual Commit	8	23
Annual Upside	20	23
Annual Prospect	33	30
Total	61	76

The overall size of the pipeline (all forecast states summed) should be growing, as should the quality of the forecast (i.e., conversion to commit). It can be seen from the first table that the pipeline at the start of the year gives an annual commit of only $8 million. By the time the team gets to the start of the second quarter, the annual commit has risen dramatically to $23 million.

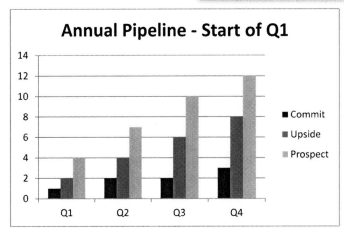

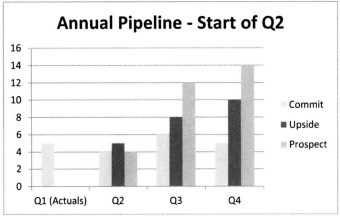

Normally, you will see small numbers of committed deals and much larger numbers associated with upsides and prospects. The deals tend to concentrate at the end of the quarter and the end of the year. Then, salespeople prefer not to come under unwanted pressure by committing; they naturally try to stay out of trouble by pushing the deals out for a long time (sandbagging).

A sales manager's job is to address this practice by working with the sales teams and customers to qualify the deals and move them through the cycle. The task is not only focused on getting the deals to the commit stage, but it's also making sure they close more rapidly. Most businesses, and especially software companies, go through hell in the final month and week of every quarter. Why? For some reason, my analysis of over 20 sales teams across multiple industries shows that 70 percent of deals close in those last three weeks. It's caused by the following factors, most of which are unhealthy for the companies:

- As mentioned, the sales teams have habitually pushed deals out as far as possible to relieve pressure. However, this means the pressure piles up at the end of a quarter, with the tension and work rate unbearably high. When this frantic period is over, everyone feels too exhausted to pick up the cudgel again with any of the vigor required. Consequently, for the first couple of weeks of the next quarter, salespeople lose momentum and tempo. They take a few weeks to get their rhythm back, then the deals that could have been closed halfway through the quarter get pushed to quarter end, and the cycle perpetuates itself. Considering everything sales managers have to address, eliminating this stop-start approach to sales would make the most appreciable difference to performance.

- Customers know their vendor and partner companies are driven by quarterly and year-end numbers. They also know the individual companies' financial-year calendars and negotiate accordingly. When vendors desperately want sales at the end of a quarter, they give discounts far more easily than at the start of a quarter. As a managing director who buys millions of dollars' worth of hardware and software every quarter, I instruct my procurement teams to wait as long as possible to place orders to coincide with vendor end-of-period dates. There's no point in booking an order halfway through a period if you know you can get an additional 5 percent discount by waiting until quarter end.

- Sales companies themselves have become hooked on the adrenaline of quarter and year ends to drive their sales forces. They depend on the buzz generated by the fear of failure and the euphoria of success. It's a totally ludicrous situation—a frenzy of discounting and giveaways to make a quarterly number that could have been achieved without the margin hit through more consistent effort. In effect, all it does is lower shareholder value for the company.

This phenomenon is best handled through strong leadership and a robust and open approach with customers. Consider these two tips:

1. Members of the sales team can't be allowed to increase and decrease their tempo of operating so abruptly. The troops need to be on the case all of the time. The best salespeople are the busy ones living on their nerves—those who can't sit still and drive hard day in and day out. While not everyone can be like this, the sales manager needs to encourage this type of approach to get the results she wants. It's about leading by example and making sure the salespeople are pushed to be extremely active. That means the sales manager is continually on the phone, out on calls, and forever demanding pipeline evolution and deal closure.

2. Sales teams need to be honest and straightforward with customers. It's simple: negotiate in a transparent way, and indicate that all of the upside the customer will get is on the table. Emphasize that, quarter end or not, the offer won't get better. If the deal doesn't close, you may just have to miss a quarter-end goal. However, customers soon face the fact that the end-of-period situation no longer factors into negotiations; they can achieve best value in the middle of a month. Now, is that so difficult?

Business Information

These days, business information is available in an increasingly wider variety of formats, thus leading to confusion about what's truly necessary. To resolve this situation, use these tools to compete in the current marketplace:

- **Online forecast tool**—Salespeople should have online access to a forecast database in which they can create and update deals. All the information previously discussed can be added in pre-formatted and free-text fields, but the critical data include five items:
  o   Customer name
  o   Deal description
  o   Projected revenue
  o   Close date
  o   Forecast state

  In companies with more than ten salespeople, allocating customers well requires discipline. The typical behavior of account managers is reprehensible when it comes to stealing customers from one another, so large businesses will need a tightly controlled list of customers. (Unfortunately, the list needs to be constantly vetted and controlled. Commonly, a salesperson will uncover an opportunity in someone else's account and reenter the customer's name on the master list with a slight variation in his or her own list of accounts (e.g., AcmeSoft, Inc. might be reentered as AcmeSoft, Ltd.). Assuming you get this right, when salespeople enter their opportunities, they will have a defined list of customers as a drop-down and won't be able to enter deals that belong to other people. If you're shocked to know this, don't be; it's how salespeople generally behave. They're aggressive and always push the rules to the limit. Channeled the right way, though, this trait can work to your advantage.

- **Online bookings**—Individual salespeople should be able to view their bookings in near-real time. This enables managers and individuals to monitor progress over the long and short term. It's important for management of the numbers and also for accuracy at the end of the period (week, month, quarter) to make sure deals are actually on the system. It can also bring a sense of drama and excitement to a team trying to close out a period. Nothing is more thrilling than seeing a deal appear. It means the end of the road (more or less) devoted to a usually torturous process of earning a purchase order from a customer.

- **Online discount tool**—Salespeople typically want to go outside of their normal discount limits to close a deal. This tendency needs to be controlled, and online tools are the best way to do it. The tool needs to provide a mechanism for asking for the discount. It also provides free-text fields to explain why it's necessary to close the deal and shows the significance of the deal in terms of overall account strategy. It's good to have a field available to describe the recovery plan (i.e., how the company will get back to normal levels of discounting with this customer because the salesperson is about to expose the possibility for the customer to achieve an unacceptably high level of discount to get the initial order. It can be very difficult to recover from this position).

The Commit Call

I strongly recommend everyone in every sales team adopt this ritual of the commit call. It's a way of pulling salespeople together at the start of the week and galvanizing them into action.

Here's how it works: Depending on the circumstances, people can be brought into the office for the meeting or they can attend over audio, Internet, or video conferencing. I like to meet at eight o'clock Monday morning after insisting the forecasting tool be updated last thing on Friday night.

When the sales manager comes in on Monday morning, he or she knows exactly where the team should be in terms of sales for the week.

People can discuss current status and determine what needs to be done to ensure the committed deals close.

Even more important is discussing the overall pipeline and (typically) the monthly and quarterly outlooks. Then the sales manager questions every individual in this open forum. This commit call can be uncomfortable for underperformers and an ideal platform for high achievers to show off. I've found it to be an incredibly effective way of driving competitive behavior, identifying stars, and weeding out the weak. As the sales manager discusses the forecast with individuals over the course of a few weeks, it becomes obvious who's on top of their business and who's struggling. The majority of the salespeople are energized by the competition. Because of that, I often find they're far more likely to get deals into their pipeline and drive them to commit and close when their peer group can openly witness their performance.

The commit call is also a chance to review what happened during the previous week—the deals that booked on schedule and, more importantly, those that didn't and why not. Usually, bookings will also arise that weren't called at all ("blue birds") as well as deals that booked earlier than committed. Although there's nothing wrong with this, be sure to get an explanation. Why didn't others know this would happen? It's often a sign of poor account control by the account manager and needs to be watched.

Later in the morning, the sales manager will go on a similar call with all of his or her peers and their sales director. A similar process will take place with the individual sales managers talking about their deals for the week, their performance last week, and the pipeline for the month and quarter.

A little later in the day, the sales director and peers will conduct a similar call with the sales VP. This way, everyone in the organization gets a feel for exactly what's happening in the business as far as sales are concerned.

Of course, in small- and medium-sized businesses, just one meeting may be adequate. But in corporations, I've seen this roll-up process to global VP be six levels deep. The principles still hold.

In every team where I've introduced the discipline and routine of the forecast and commit calls, I've experienced the following results:

Commit Calls—A Waste of Time or Highly Valuable?

A lot of salespeople say insisting on a commit call is a phenomenal waste of time. Why drag people into meetings when they could be out in the field selling? And why do it every week? After all, things don't change that much over seven days, right?

I certainly understand these comments coming from the uninitiated. Their point of view from the outside makes sense to them because they've never experienced the power generated by a weekly cycle of forecasting and commit calls. Yet, my experience has been consistently positive.

- **Sales increase**—Regular improvements of 50 percent in sales revenues and occasionally astonishing growth rates of nearly 400 percent when teams are driven to forecast and commit on a weekly basis.

- **Increased Competitiveness**—Salespeople all want to appear as heroes on the calls and never want to be seen as failures when their big talk doesn't materialize. So they self regulate and fight to outdo each other. This creates the high-tempo whirlwind of activity and competition that not only drives numbers but increases the dynamism and productivity of the team.

- **Awareness of individual deals**—I'm often taken aback by how little knowledge there is inside companies about significant pieces of business. This situation is usually due to two things: (1) a poor forecasting solution that prevents transparency and (2) a propensity for salespeople to keep big chunks of business secret—the sandbagger approach. By having the high-tempo forecast regime, though, this simply can't happen. Whenever I implement more stringent forecasting, executives tune into deals and get involved personally in trying to make them happen. Most salespeople cringe at this, but that's nonsensical. Stringent forecasting produces a massive benefit to get the company's leadership on the trail of new business. It also attracts attention, engagement, and resources, which all lead to eventual success.

- **Early identification of resource requirements**—Built into the forecast process is identifying additional presales, development, and financial resources to get the deal done. You may be familiar with the scramble that generally takes place at the last minute and the bitter recriminations of failure when salespeople can't get those they need to the meetings they've booked. Early warning is the key, and the forecast addresses this well. Salespeople with significant deals who need assistance can get resources scheduled well ahead of time. (Yes, I realize customers rarely adhere to timetables buried in the free-text fields of the forecast. But trust me; the very fact that salespeople are talking about their requirements early means they have a better chance of getting the help they need when they need it than if they send out a panicky voice mail two days before they need a top development engineer in Hong Kong.)

- **Company-wide momentum**—Forecasting is not just about the sales team, of course. Production and development teams benefit massively from early visibility of deals. And finance can glean huge gains from correctly predicting numbers for communication to company stakeholders (particularly the stock market) and understanding cash-flow needs as the period progresses. But more than that, the benefit stems from everyone rallying around a forecast. Personnel from the shop floor to the boardroom start to talk about the numbers and how the company is progressing toward its order intake, revenue, and profit targets. Everyone feels part of the success of the greater team.

Yes, you *can* gain a lot of benefit from a simple forecast process. But to succeed in achieving these benefits, leaders have to overtly commit to the new process—to attend meetings religiously and insist on the accuracy of the numbers and documents produced. Good sales managers hold their salespeople accountable in these meetings to expose and eliminate poor forecasting, low levels of commitment, and shaky knowledge of customers and deals.

I can't recommend highly enough the power of the commit call and forecast as well as adopting the planning process based on tested business and military principles. Sales teams and their leaders can garner extensive benefits from a considered, disciplined approach to the planning and organizational effort.

Conclusion

Planning for sales involves a continuum of activities by sales operations, which provides the core of the effort—from the creation of the vision and strategy and the consequent planning all the way down to account manager level. With that in place, leaders are wise to manage teams through the use of the forecast, the pipeline, business information, and the commit call. When all components are orchestrated properly and executed by highly motivated sales teams, the results are overwhelmingly good.

2   Selection and Maintenance of Objectives

You ask, what is our aim? I can answer in one word. It is victory. Victory at all costs.—**Winston Churchill**, *British prime minister*

Management by objective works—if you know the objectives. Ninety percent of the time you don't.—**Peter Drucker**, *American business guru*

You often hear the expression "If you don't know where you're going, any road will take you there"—and it's quite true. You'd be amazed at the number of sales teams I encounter that have no clue what's expected of them or, worse still, have no belief in the objectives they've been given.

It's heartbreaking to come across salespeople drifting aimlessly through their days, making random calls, and passing uncertain messages to customers. It's demoralizing for the individuals involved, wasteful at best and damaging at worst for the employing company, and a tragic waste of human endeavor.

I also hear the same people say, "We've got no chance of making the number this year; right now, it's all about setting ourselves up for next year." In other words, they know they won't make their targets in the current financial year. As a result, they're holding back deals for the following period, when their target will be lower based on a poor performance in the current year.

However you look at it, a sales team that's aimless, unsure of where it's supposed to be positioning, demotivated by unrealistic order intake targets, or a mixture of all three provides a recipe for disaster.

I'm a strong believer in the maxim that all deserve to be told what's expected of them and then told how they're performing against those expectations. That's important, but I offer a further caveat: there's no

The eventual failure of Operation Barbarossa, the German invasion of Russia in 1941, is often blamed on Hitler's inability to select and maintain an objective. The Germans had advanced into Russia with characteristic speed and success on three key fronts with Army Groups North, Central, and South. Hitler wanted to take Moscow with Army Group Central, but he diverted the Fourth Panzer Army from the center to Army Group South to assist in the encirclement at Kiev. Likewise, he diverted large numbers of resources to Army Group North to take Leningrad. The Germans became bogged down in Leningrad and lost a great deal of men and materiel in Kiev. Indeed, Hitler changed his aim at Leningrad from invasion and rapid victory to siege and starving out.

When Operation Typhoon, the attack on Moscow, finally did get underway, the overstretching of the army, lack of manpower and transport, and the coming of winter led to failure and the survival of the city. Had Hitler made the capture of Moscow the key objective of Operation Barbarossa, plenty of evidence suggests he would have been successful. Instead, multiple and changing objectives caused dilution of the effort and eventual defeat.

point setting goals for salespeople that are unrealistic and perceived to be unachievable.

This becomes the greatest challenge of all for sales leaders: how do I set a goal that's achievable but stretching and, at the same time, doesn't demotivate people?

Most people have heard of SMART objectives or goals. SMART is an acronym for specific, measurable, achievable, results-oriented,* and time bound. This may be an old formula, but it's a great framework to use when setting your objectives. That said, as you sit down with your blank sheet of paper and sharpened pencils to start this exercise, consider the following:

- Establish a clear idea of the market size and, more importantly, what your customers (and potential customers) are doing in the coming twelve months. This type of data will come from your own team, the media, market analysts, and intelligence that you

---

*   *Results-oriented* is often written as *realistic*, but from a sales perspective, I prefer *results-oriented* because *realistic* is similar to *achievable*.

glean from the marketplace—that is, from talking to customers, attending trade shows, and so on. Your market knowledge must be continually refined, requiring you to frequently revisit your plans. You need to know (1) the size of the projects, (2) the timing of the order and revenue being recognized, (3) the products and services your company will provide if you win the business, and (4) any investments your company might need to make to win it.

- Create brand-new opportunities. Don't fall into the trap of letting customers plan the business through their intentions. Rather, decide how you can generate business in the market that the customer doesn't yet know about or have a line for in the budget. This is what makes good teams great—generating opportunities unique to the sales team and its customer. Wouldn't it be sales nirvana if a customer realized you and only you have the product or service that solves the customer's issues and gives that company a profitable, competitive advantage? Even though it's never quite like that, this point remains: when you plan, make sure you feed in fresh, out-of-the-box ideas to encourage your sales teams not only to respond to customer enquiries and plans but also to generate brand-new opportunities. Create demand. You're not driving your business onward and upward if you're only responding to established customer projects.

- Know what the company is doing in product and service development, and become prepared to market new developments. To do a good job, a sales leader needs to have a clear idea about what will likely succeed and then works with the product and marketing teams to develop offerings that will sell. As you set objectives for your sales teams, make sure you take into account the need to both introduce and sell these new products. There's nothing more embarrassing than having lobbied hard to get a new product or service introduced only to learn that members of the sales team can't, won't, or don't sell it.

- Know what's going on in marketing (advertising, expos, mailings, Internet, social media, call outs, etc.) and when these activities are scheduled to be implemented. Then coordinate your sales efforts with campaigns, while ensuring the objectives you're setting for the salespeople are fully supported by a coordinated marketing effort. In a successful company, the grand plan pulls all of the elements together in a seamless fusion of coordinated activity.

Let's return to those SMART objectives and discuss what sales managers need to think about to allocate objectives to their troops.

First, a word to the wise: sales objectives aren't only about order intake numbers. I know plenty of salespeople who say it doesn't matter what you do as long as you bring in the number. Personally, I'm a big numbers person, so I always focus on the numbers—weekly, monthly, and quarterly. Indeed, as you've seen, the forecast is central to everything a sales team does, but you have to be careful. You typically get what you measure, and if you're not mindful of the dangers, you'll end up with a sales team that's close to harassing its customers for orders. They may not give thought to addressing their customers' principle concerns, building long-term relationships, carrying out deep discovery to get under the hood of the customers' businesses, and working to be a long-term business partner. The result? The salesperson thrashes numbers out of customers for twelve months, and you get the results you wanted, but customers feel abused and even look elsewhere. You always want to build long-term relationships with your customers, not milk them for every penny they've got.

The psychology of driving a number in this smash-and-grab fashion encourages even worse behaviors. A lot of clients allude to the fact that salespeople from an unloved supplier are all over them when there's a purchase to be made. But once the purchase order is signed, they never see the salesperson again.

The best way to understand how this feels is to empathize with the customer, to put yourself in the buyer's place, like in this scenario: You put faith in a supplier. You probably take a risk to use that supplier because if the purchase doesn't provide the value expected, it leads to embarrassment, losses, and career setbacks. You work to get budget allocated and contracts processed. Then, all of a sudden, the person you thought would partner with you disappears.

How would you feel? Not good. So as a sales manager, you have to stop the type of behavior that can be generated by giving salespeople purely numbers-based targets.

But wait a minute. I hear a plaintive cry from the traditionalists: "Good salespeople know that they live and die by relationships. They know that smash-and-grab is incredibly short-term and lands you in trouble in the long run."

News flash—if you base your actions on the premise that all salespeople are sensible and good and that you can rely on them to behave responsibly, then you're in for a series of nasty surprises. Although it may damage your faith in human nature, you have to accept that compensation drives behavior. If you set a suite of objectives and associated compensation based solely on order intake numbers, then your chances of building lasting relationships with your customers are slim.

Also watch out for the mistake sales leaders often make. They focus on pure order intake and forget about profit levels and cash collections. That's what makes this statement true: "Revenue is for vanity; profit is for sanity." Given flexibility in pricing and one-dimensional objectives, salespeople can destroy your margins before you know it.

If you're coaching your people to act as account managers, that also means they need to ensure that cash is being collected in a timely fashion. It's the dirty end of a less-than-glamorous job, but it needs to be done. So set your objectives accordingly.

Having been through the planning process, you have a product and service plan. You also have a clear idea how that plan fits in with your marketing activities for the period. You want to give your salespeople a set of objectives that not only meets your revenue, profit, and cash-flow goals but also provides for a burgeoning long-term relationship with your customers.

SMART Objectives

It's a cool acronym—specific, measurable, achievable, results-oriented, and time bound—but what does that mean? Essentially, for every objective you set for a salesperson, you need to be able to check off five boxes indicating that each of the SMART criterion has been met.

Specific

This means that you must specifically indicate what's required of the salesperson. You may ask, how specific do I need to be? What's the danger of micromanaging to such a degree that I simply can't cope with the volume of detail I have asked for? If I do, will the salesperson feel demotivated because his or her initiative is effectively stymied?

It's difficult to be prescriptive. It depends on the salespeople themselves, your relationship with them, and their ability to interpret your requirements. So to ease the explanation around objective setting, here's an example to act as a framework:

> A sales team has a new account it wants to penetrate—a public sector customer called Ministry of Works (MoW) in an unnamed country. The team knows MoW has a $20 million budget for the year to improve both the size and power of its computers and the network that joins them together. The sales team has calculated it can secure $3 million of that budget, even though it currently has no account with the organization.
>
> The sales manager needs to be specific when setting this objective. "Sell $3 million of compute and network capability to MoW" is a start, but it's too simplistic to be of much use. An alternative objective would be "Sell $3 million of compute and network to MoW by building relationships with the CIO and his department and by creating a common plan for success."

That's specific in terms of what the sales manager wants from a revenue perspective and includes softer information. But how can we measure the relationship build?

Measurable

The first half of the objective referring to revenue is clear and easy to measure. The manager then adds this text that hardens the numerical objective and puts more measurability into the softer part of the objective:

Sell $3 million of compute and network to MoW at a minimum contribution margin of 10 percent by building relationships with the CIO and his department and creating a common plan for success. Relationship building will culminate in an executive briefing at our premises for the CIO and his team, with a written plan detailing MoW's requirements and our plans to fulfill them.

The sales manager is able to measure performance against this objective. She knows the target-order intake and the target margin (and price). And she's also told the salesperson to think about the relationship build and put together a briefing and plan addressing MoW's issues.

She's been specific and put a measurement matrix in place but hasn't been overly prescriptive. The salesperson can look at the customer landscape and start working on how to build relationships with MoW's CIO and his department. He'll have to call dozens of people, drink gallons of coffee, and schedule and reschedule untold numbers of meetings. Over the course of all that, he'll be putting together a set of converging stories about MoW's issues and requirements and then matching them with his own company's capabilities. Thus, a long-term relationship is being developed.

This centers on giving salespeople more than a number to chase. They're being measured on something softer but just as important—relationship build. If the sales manager doesn't approach it like this, she'll face the possibility that her sales team will default to calling the MoW procurement department, asking about the purchase schedule, and seeing how they can compete. (Yes, the procurement people will look to see who the lowest-cost vendor is.) Worse still, if the salespeople see no opportunities in the procurement plan, they'll disqualify MoW from their calling schedule. And there you have it. Poor objective setting will have led the company totally out of the MoW partner environment.

So far in our example, the objective is specific and measurable. What's next?

Achievable

This is the tricky one—objective setting's *schwerpunkt*.[†] As a matter of course, salespeople will tell you that you, as the sales manager, have given them too big a number that can't be reached. In the same way, customers always say your price is too high. Is a salesperson ever going to tell you to give a *bigger* number? Will a customer ever demand you *raise* your price? Of course not. So understand that you'll eventually have to tell the salesperson, "That's your objective, and it won't change." And you'll have to tell a customer, "That's the best price we can give."

But you need to know what you're doing because if you set unachievable objectives, you'll set off a chain of events that could result in disaster. First, you'll encourage bad behavior with the customer. At one extreme, the salesperson will give up on the account and look to profit elsewhere. At the other extreme, the salesperson will start to unreasonably batter the customer to get orders, leading to customer disaffection. Overall, you risk creating morale and retention problems—not just with the individual salesperson but often with the entire team.

There's no alternative to discovering and understanding what's going on in the market. I call it "the GOYA principle." This term has nothing to do with Spanish painters; GOYA stands for "Get Off Your A**" (i.e., backside). You need to get yourself into the market to find out what's going on. As a sales manager, you need to develop relationships with customers, partners, distributors, and so forth to obtain an ever-evolving picture of where the potential lies. What are the customers' pain points? What is the competition doing? And, most important, what sales numbers are available with your existing and potential customers? Find out.

I hear two myths from salespeople all the time, paraphrased as follows:

1. "Please don't interfere with my work. Just tell me my number and let me get on with it. If I fail, you can get rid of me."

---

† *Schwerpunkt* is a German word meaning point of focus or point of concentrated activity, often used by the military in conjunction with the principles of blitzkrieg.

2. "I don't want to take you to my customers because once they meet you and get your mobile number, they won't want to talk to me; they'll only call you."

This is pure nonsense. Don't accept this type of positioning from salespeople. They "own" the accounts on your behalf, but the customers buy from the company; therefore, you're all responsible for success. You're also responsible to make sure *you* know the customers well as you ensure your account manager is doing a good job. You need to be involved in the account, meeting the customers and discussing their issues.

Do be careful not to undermine account managers. Make sure they're the ones who pick up actions and remain at the fulcrum of your accounts. If possible, avoid customer meetings without the account manager present. And don't fall into the trap of sorting out problems on your own. Keep delegating activity to the salesperson/account manager.

Also beware of calling a salesperson and saying, "I'm coming into town, so arrange for me to see some customers." That's pointless. Why? It smacks of having a hole in your diary, needing to be seen in the market, and tasking the salespeople to arrange empty visits that have no sensible objectives. Instead, talk to your salespeople over time and work out where you can add value in their accounts.

That's how it works from an intelligence point of view. You'll be able to set an achievable objective a lot more credibly if you know exactly what's going on.

In addition, you'll be able to look at past performance, both in the specific account for which you're setting objectives and in similar accounts. Past performance often indicates future results, so applying this knowledge will help you set achievable objectives.

As noted at the beginning of this section, it's tough to get objective setting right, and no one will thank you for setting objectives, whatever they are. However, your best bet is to research the situation well and deliver the news to the salespeople with confidence and optimism. Don't catch yourself saying, "There's nothing I can do; this number's been passed down to me from country level." That almost guarantees you'll shatter morale before you even start the sales period.

When you come to tabulate objectives, it's sensible to explain why you believe the objective is achievable (e.g., the customer has budget available, there's a growing requirement for a solution to a particular issue, and the like). This makes it more difficult for the salesperson to push back. Compare this approach with the reaction you'll get if you simply send an e-mail that spells out a large target number. That's not exactly inspirational leadership!

Results-Oriented

As said earlier in the book, "If you don't know where you're going, any road will take you there." That means you need to know exactly what results you're looking for when you set objectives. It also may mean planning for a horizon further out than twelve months.

Let's look at a few planned outcomes and how this affects objective setting.

Sales managers typically receive a profit-and-revenue target from their board or management. It likely gives little detail beyond specifying a number and profit level, a geographical limit, and (if they're lucky) a product/service mix.

No matter how senior your position in an organization, always pass as much detail as you can down the hierarchy. It's demoralizing and unhelpful for teams to have only numbers handed to them, so always convey the holistic plan in your downward communications.

Here's an example of how this would work in practice.

A sales manager gets a number for her territory of $100 million at a gross margin level of 10 percent. That's it—no more detail. But her plan calls for this set of additional objectives:

- Penetrate the MoW account where the team is not currently present.

- Gain 10 percent more sales of data-center switching.

- Grow existing accounts by 15 percent.

- Capture four new accounts to generate revenue of $2 million each in the first year.

As a business leader, the sales manager needs to add intelligence to the process. If she has a team of four account managers, the temptation is to give them $25 million each and divide the named accounts among them. In 90 percent of cases using this approach, the manager would be setting up the team to fail. Some account managers will overachieve, and others will underachieve. Why? Because no thought was given to identifying the lucrative accounts versus those being developed. The number should be divided among the account managers accordingly. In addition, with this crude approach, the sales manager has lost the chance to achieve planned results through objective setting.

Sales managers can apply a results orientation to objective setting. Normally, objective setting for salespeople is based on twelve-month revenue and profit plans. However, a results orientation provides an opportunity for leaders to inject longer-term planning with results expectations noted in the shorter-term annual objectives.

So let's add wording (shown in italics) to our sample objective to reflect a results orientation:

> Sell $3 million of compute and network, *including $400k of data center switching*, to MoW at a minimum contribution margin of 10 percent by building relationships with the CIO and his department and creating a common plan for success. Relationship building will culminate in an executive briefing at our premises for the CIO and his team. It includes a written plan detailing MoW's requirements and our plans to fulfill them.

Yes, the objective is becoming a bit of a mouthful now, but don't despair. We'll revisit this issue when we look at how objectives get tabulated in a more readable and executable way. But next, let's consider the simplest of the SMART objectives.

Time Bound

How hard can it be to put a time limit on an objective? "Sell $25 million at 10 percent gross profit by year-end" would be a classic directive. Nevertheless, you should consider two important aspects.

First, as a manager, you'll typically have a mixture of hard and soft objectives. You've already seen that you need to make these objectives measurable in terms of tangible results. It makes sense to inject timing into the matrix so you know at what point you need to check for success. You don't want to leave monitoring your teams until a deliverable is due; constant monitoring with the end point and deadline in mind is critical.

Second, as described earlier, it's important to coordinate sales objectives with marketing campaigns, product introductions, and manufacturing logistics. It's much better to drive data-center switching sales at the same time as the launching of a related marketing campaign. Always seek to maximize the impact of resources by acting in a coordinated way.

Let's take this wordy objective and make it time bound:

Sell $3 million of compute and network, including $400k of data-center switching, to MoW *by year-end* at a minimum contribution margin of 10 percent by building relationships with the CIO and his department and creating a common plan for success. Relationship building will culminate in an executive briefing *during Q2* at our premises for the CIO and his team, with a written plan detailing MoW's requirements and our plans to fulfill them to be published *by the end of Q2*.

SMART Objective Tabulation

The objective looks good, but one thing is missing. in general, salespeople don't like to read, and they certainly don't like to read complicated things. They will say, "I now understand what you need from me." Then they will ask, "But how am I going to get paid?" This doesn't make them greedy and dirty; it's just how they are.

I've developed the following matrix that enables managers to clearly specify expectations to the salesperson. It also assists leaders in matching objectives to compensation plans. (You'll read more about that in chapter 5.)

Table 2.1
Matrix for Ministry of Works (MoW) Objective
Account Manager: Angela
Objective: 1

Sub-Objective	Specific	Measureable	Achievable	Results Oriented	Time-bound	Achievement
a	Sell total $3 million of compute and network at 10% contribution margin (CM).	$3 million at 10% CM	MoW ICT budget is $20 million this year and it has data center requirements.	MoW is a new target customer.	By year-end	
b	Sell $400k of DC switching at 10% CM.	$400k at 10% CM	MoW is extending its DCs this year.	Sell 10% of total team revenue as DC switching.	Sale in Q3 to track Web and press campaign on DC switching in Q2.	
c	Arrange executive briefing with CIO team.	Briefing takes place.	We know the CIO is eager to build partner relations.	Achieve CIO partnership and MoW account penetration.	During Q2	
d	Produce written plan detailing MoW requirements and our approach to meeting those objectives.	Report production in a fit-for-purpose fashion.	We know the CIO is amenable to building this type of framework.	Provides matrix for our relationship and penetration of MoW.	End of Q2	

The "achieved" column on the right in the table provides a clue about how this method can be used to measure success. From a compensation perspective, this column is useful at the end of the period. It's easy enough to see if the salesperson has met her objectives and pay her accordingly. That's all well and good, but let's make sure we have a way to monitor progress and maintain objectives. We want to keep the team moving in line with the objectives and achieve the plan.

Maintaining Sales Objectives

It's surprisingly easy to lose sight of objectives almost as soon as they're set. Priorities change, unexpected events occur, and people lose their focus.

I deal with sales teams every day, and it's quite common for them to have no clear idea about the objectives they're expected to achieve.

How do we overcome this common problem of objective drift and subsequent loss of focus?

Communication

First, objectives as laid out in this chapter need to be distributed in a way that people understand what they are, how they will be measured, and how they fit in to the overall plan. Too often, this communication devolves into handing out goal sheets, a bit of a consequent negotiation around the individual numbers, and an eventual showdown in which either the account managers sign up for their targets or go into protracted conflict with the leadership team. You won't be surprised to discover I've got a few issues with this approach!

As mentioned earlier, having a sole focus on the number is a mistake. Of course, setting a numerable objective is an important part of the process, but what's paramount is the overall set of objectives. You'll want to discuss this more holistic approach with the salespeople and use it as context for the numbers you communicate.

In a perfectly frictionless environment, the salesperson and the manager will be as one in terms of the objectives and the size of the numeric target. In reality, this is rarely the case, but skillful sales management will result in a process that's nonconfrontational, if not painless.

I can't emphasize enough the importance of getting your team to buy into your objectives. If the salespeople only want to fight about the number, you'll have problems. However, if the sales team becomes engaged with the broader set of objectives, that deeper involvement will ultimately drive growth far more effectively.

A strong element of persuasion and consensus building works most effectively when allocating objectives and targets. E-mailing an objective sheet to each salesperson is unlikely to achieve a resounding acceptance. Why? Because individuals need face-to-face time to discuss objectives, voice concerns, and ultimately sign up for the plan.

Often, the account manager has been in the account a long time and presumes to know more than you. All sales managers have likely heard comments like these: "You don't understand how Acme does business. You can't just breeze in and sell like that." If you've been acting on the GOYA principle advocated earlier, you'll know how Acme does business. Then you can credibly say to the bold salesperson, "Actually, I disagree. The last time I spoke to the CIO... ." At this point, you've won the argument. From then on in, you can have a sensible conversation around the objective. But do bear in mind, if you're the kind of manager who spends the bulk of her time in the corner office staring at a spreadsheet, you're coming from a tougher position when you work to persuade/ cajole/motivate those on your teams.

On other occasions, you'll be talking to people who are moving into new accounts. In these circumstances, I'd highly advise you not to give these account managers big (and possibly unachievable) targets, or you risk setting them up for failure. Then you'll have morale problems, and, more worrisome, you'll have a demotivated individual representing your cause to your customers—never a good thing. So do your best to set reasonable objectives for new account managers; then encourage individuals to go out and make it happen.

Shared Objectives

Part of the psychology of communicating objectives well is to convey the feeling to the salesperson that you share the objectives. From that person's perspective, there's nothing worse than feeling hung out to dry with a difficult set of tasks while the rest of the team has an easy ride. It's more motivating for the account manager to feel you're in this together—that you, as the sales manager, have bought into the objectives and are dedicated to working together to achieve them.

Discussing the objectives face to face is essential. Once you've agreed they make sense, you can move forward. I recommend that you print them off in duplicate and both sign the copies, which you retain for the year. This sounds old-fashioned in our click-to-accept world, but sometimes these tactile experiences add to a sense of theater. This can make the occasion seem far more memorable and of greater importance.

So you've communicated the objectives in a face-to-face, consultative, and tactile way. The troops know what they have to do for the next twelve months. Next, you need to monitor progress.

Monitoring

Despite your hard work, the salesperson will likely carry on exactly as before the meeting with little thought to the objectives on the signed paper. I've worked in sales from Singapore to Seattle, and for whatever reason, salespeople the world over have the retention span of forgetful goldfish. If you know why this is, do tell me!

I surmise the main problem is they're highly focused on a specific set of numbers and deals, and they find everything else a distraction. In some ways, this can be good, but you won't maximize your impact with customers if you allow them to get away with it.

Even as you're discussing the objectives, you need to convey the message that you'll be reviewing the progress every two weeks. Why two weeks? More frequently will burden you too much; any longer interval won't be effective.

Now, inevitably, as you review the objectives, you'll come up with a set of actions you need to monitor to achieve the desired results. Salespeople need to own these actions, tabulate them, and add to them as they go about their business. The following chart provides an example of what I mean.

Table 2.2
Actions Toward Meeting Sales Objectives
Account: MoW
Account Manager: Angela
Objective: 1

Sub-Objective	Action	Comments	Timeline
la	Provide high-level design for data center network.	CIO interested in our DC technology and needs an overview of how we could meet his objectives.	Aug. 14
lb	Engage presales engineer for discussion with head of campus networks.	Customer has issues with network coverage inside the campus.	Aug. 30
lc	Book dates for executive briefing at HQ.	CIO has given us prospective dates for the briefing.	Sept. 15
lc	Book speakers for the briefing.	Need experts on DC, campus switching, and wireless.	Sept. 15

Monitoring sessions are highly important to ensure salespeople are covering all bases to get the objectives met. Although it's an exhaustive process that may raise accusations of micromanagement, in the majority of cases, not only is it helpful, but it's essential to maintain your sales objectives. It comes down to a matter of style and experience. You'll undoubtedly have strong performers who won't react kindly to this type of high-touch management, and you can lighten up in these cases but give additional guidance in others.

You'll find this consultative approach far more effective when compared with instructions like "You need to make four sales calls a day and provide visit reports on each one, and I'll be checking your online diary." Unfortunately, this technique is well-known—along with its unpleasant corollaries, such as calling a salesperson at 8:00 AM to tell her you'll be accompanying her on her calls that day. This kind of method is both punitive and ineffective.

Even though a high-touch style of monitoring is time-consuming and requires hard work, it beats the alternatives when striving to meet your objectives.

Flexibility

The military has a saying that "no plan survives first contact with the enemy." Are you familiar with that sinking feeling you can get after outlining your carefully crafted account plan for the year to a prospective company's CIO, only to hear, "Well, that's not really what we had in mind." Back to the old drawing board.

You need to find a flexible approach to what you're doing—and modify your objectives as circumstances change. I'm not suggesting you change them in response to a salesperson saying a number is unachievable. That's a recipe for chaos. Rather, you want to modify your aim as your customers alter their plans. They will change priorities throughout the year, modify budgets (always down, for some reason), and launch new initiatives. Be sure to keep abreast of these kinds of changes.

I chatted with a VP from a big network manufacturing organization about this. He said his company conducts an objective-setting exercise at the start of the year, but its leaders never look at those objectives again until year-end. This isn't a stated policy; the company simply doesn't emphasize them. Because so much changes over twelve months, it was amazing how little relevance those January 1 objectives bore to what actually happened during the year. And that will always happen in a fast-moving, globalized economy. If you adopt the "set and forget" approach to objectives, you might as well not bother with them.

Conclusion

Setting SMART objectives provide an excellent way of creating and tabulating goals that are specific, measurable, achievable, results-oriented, and time bound. They leave no room for confusion as they translate plans into executable actions. When set properly, they are intensely motivating for sales teams while providing matrices to help management monitor progress.

Three keys to maintaining objectives are as follows:

1. **Communication**—Communicate in an empathetic way and coown the objectives with the salesperson. Make sure you both sign off on a paper document to add to the impact of this tactile experience.

2. **Monitoring**—Hold reviews of progress every two weeks. Make sure the account manager builds and owns an "actions" list so you can monitor progress in a granular way.

3. **Flexibility**—The customer environment will change, so while maintaining your overall objectives, adapt to these changing circumstances or risk seeing your objectives become irrelevant.

You've identified what you and your team will be doing. Now take offensive action with gusto!

3 Offensive Action

If you wage war, do it energetically and with severity.—**Napoleon Bonaparte,** *French general and politician*

If you're attacking your market from multiple positions and your competition isn't, you have all the advantage and it will show up in your increased success and income.—**Jay Abraham**, *marketing expert*

For team members, the idea of offensive action produces the feeling they're getting off on the right foot, driving into the market, and pushing the value proposition to their customers. It creates an atmosphere of positivity, high morale, and confidence that inevitably leads to results. Teams can then obliterate what had previously been barriers to progress, sweep aside problems, and roll up the score.

Sounds great, doesn't it? But what exactly is "offensive action" as it relates to the sales environment? Let's break it down, starting with the sales leader.

Role of the Sales Leader

This fact is critical: if the leader of the sales team, at any level, demonstrates negativity or pessimism, it's like a highly contagious virus that affects the whole team within hours. Very quickly, heads go down and watercooler chats center on *why*—why the team is doing badly, why customers aren't buying, why products aren't up to expectations, why marketing's doing a poor job, and so on. It's deadly.

As a sales leader, you have a massive responsibility to engender a can-do attitude in the team and generate what I call "offensive spirit."

There isn't a better example of offensive action being executed in war than Operation Overlord, the D-Day landings in 1944. Well before the invasion of France, the Allies had pounded German supply chains and the Luftwaffe into a beleaguered state through intensive air attack. They had also undermined enemy morale through psychological operations and engaged in deception by feigning attacks on multiple fronts.

The landings themselves took place over a wide area and in depth. Airborne and parachute troops achieved deep penetration, while massive concentration of force included airborne and seaborne bombardment and armored assault on the beaches. After the landings, the breakout attacks were carried out at high tempo, employing overwhelming air superiority. General Eisenhower acted like a football coach, traveling up and down the line, encouraging fast-moving, intense offensive action.

Offensive Spirit

Sales forces all work in complicated environments with many moving parts. Our organizations are complex mixes of engineering, manufacturing, delivery, finance, services, legal support, marketing, and general management. Couple this with the fact that many organizations are globalized, with teams operating across the world. This makes the old-fashioned meeting where leaders could gather people and strategize together impossible.

A salesperson's life is further complicated by the fact that customers are nearly always uncooperative, inconsistent, and difficult to deal with (which customers see as part of their job when interacting with salespeople). This tendency is rarely recognized inside your own company; it's always seen as a failing of the sales team when customers are behaving in an uncooperative fashion.

The point is, it's difficult to get things done (both internally and externally) and quite easy for team members to lose heart and momentum while solving problems on their customers' behalf.

This is where offensive spirit comes in. As a leader, you simply can't afford to accept that immovable barriers to moving forward exist. You need to remain relentless in your drive to bring home the sales objectives—to be aggressive in your pursuit of new opportunities—despite the gaggle of doubters who will tell you it can't be done. Be constantly cheerful and optimistic, suggesting ways to solve problems while making calls and presentations to customers and team members, especially when momentum fades. Just as negativity is contagious, so is offensive spirit. If you treat every problem as solvable, aggressively attack each challenge, and seize every sensible opportunity, your team will follow suit. Don't accept the type of self-pitying defeatism that ruins morale and invariably leads to failure.

That said, nobody is Superman or Wonder Woman. You'll have mornings when you face setbacks, you're not feeling 100 percent, and a lot of seemingly insurmountable challenges lie ahead. But you're a leader of salespeople; you have to be relentless. You need to walk into the office or get on the first call of the day with a big smile and a determination to solve every problem that comes your way. More than that, your job is to encourage your people to get out there and look for, address, and win new opportunities.

Tough? Absolutely.

I know a senior VP in a US computer company who told me he can sense when he walks into a team meeting from the buzz (or lack of it) how well the team is being led and consequently performing. A well-motivated team is chattering and laughing, happy to engage with newcomers. They demonstrate an authentic feeling of positivity and a can-do attitude—an offensive spirit.

On the contrary, a poorly motivated and failing team will be quiet. People will be self-absorbed and will generally avoid eye contact. A feeling of apprehension will fill the air, and these individuals won't appear to be a team at all.

Keep in mind that this negative state of mind is contagious not only within the company but among customers as well. No one wants to talk to a dull, seemingly disinterested, demotivated salesperson. A customer can sense if a person is likely to be boring, void of ideas, a time waster, and a negative influence. With that mindset infecting your team, will you win any orders?

Yes, low morale is a leadership issue; it's your challenge. So get among the team members and foster an offensive spirit. If you do that successfully, nothing can stop you and your team.

Seize the Initiative

Let's say you've done a good job and showing offensive spirit is the order of the day. What next?

Business is all about opportunity. Even in the deepest recessions, you can find openings to sell. The dynamics of the moment may be for rapid expansion of IT as in the heady days of the late 1990s or for major cost savings as experienced from 2008 onward. Whatever the situation, opportunities abound for the resourceful and imaginative salesperson.

Members of an effective sales team will have their plans and objectives clarified. Then they will talk frequently to CxO-level customers about issues they're experiencing in their businesses. They know every one of those conversations will spark an inkling of an opportunity. With any luck, by speaking to a lot of customers, a pattern will emerge that allows the team to launch an initiative on multiple fronts.

First, however, ensure your team members are speaking to the right people. This allows them to seize the initiative—one of the more controversial aspects of selling. You may often hear the phrase "call high," meaning "have conversations with those in the CxO suite." That's when you find out what's going on in a company and can therefore uncover opportunities.

Yes, that's a good strategy. But you have to be careful about "calling high" due to pitfalls like these:

- It's difficult to get an appointment at a high level without extensive knowledge of the company. You need to show relevance to the success of the company's customers before anyone will consider helping you to get an appointment with a CxO. That requires a salesperson to do considerable groundwork with middle management before it's possible to land the opportunity to talk to a senior executive.

- If you try to get a high-level call too quickly, you run the risk of upsetting key managers in the middle of the company. They might feel slighted because you have jumped over them. So put yourself in their place. It would definitely feel unpleasant for their contact (you) to go straight to the CxO. To be smart, make it advantageous for your middle management contacts to have you visit the CxO level. Surprisingly, you'll often find it's much easier for you as a vendor/supplier/partner to get in front of an executive than it is for employees. You can use this advantage to help middle managers fulfill their goals by acting as the ambassador into the CxO suite.

- Let's say you do get an early CxO appointment and, because you don't have enough background, you mess it up. Not only does this waste time in meeting your immediate objectives, but you can burn your reputation with the executive, his or her colleagues, and the middle managers who helped you. That makes it extremely tough to get an appointment later.

Pass those warnings and suggestions on to your salespeople so they will go about obtaining a high-level visit in the most effective way. And once they've obtained the appointment, prepare them to detect opportunity in an executive conversation. Be aggressive and confident enough to follow through on any opening they uncover.

I can't overemphasize how vital it is to have this offensive spirit inculcated into your teams. Every week, I see salespeople make disastrous mistakes in customer meetings by not spotting an opening or being too negative to exploit it. When preparing for important meetings, salespeople often use phrases like these:

"We have to make sure we set expectations correctly."

"We need to make sure we don't overcommit."

"We've tried that before, and it didn't work."

"I doubt that's going to be possible."

These statements reveal an underlying propensity to say no—and should never be in the playbook of offensively oriented teams.

This leads to another controversial area—hundreds of outraged sales leaders saying, "Overpromising is the curse of selling. When you do it, you lose your customers by disappointing them."

No doubt you've heard stories about VPs promising the world to companies, then going mysteriously silent and leaving the account team responsible. Clearly, you have to find the right balance. But if you are in a CxO-level meeting, realize you won't get repeat opportunities, so, for heaven's sake, seize the moment.

These real-life examples can show you how. After explaining the situation, I play out two scenarios for each one: (1) an offensive approach and (2) the more usual negative, opportunity-killing putdown.

Real Life Example 1

In this classic situation for a hardware vendor, I visited the CTO of a Russian telecommunications service provider that had an account team in Moscow. My contacts had good relations in the account and easy access to the executives—a great sign. Sales were lower than they should have been by about 50 percent. This percentage took into play the size of the service provider and the company's benchmarks for similar-sized accounts in the region.

As always, the CTO was facing a lot of challenges. He told us he needed a level of discount that, frankly, our company would never be able to provide.

Negative Scenario—What Could Have Happened

At this point, the team members looked at each other nervously and let it be known they were already giving the CTO the best discount they could. They simply couldn't do any better. Worse still, they revealed they have an internal process that dictated discounts, saying the CTO's request would never be approved.

The CTO wasn't an arch villain wanting to trick his way to deeper discounts. (Most people just don't think that way.) Rather, he had real challenges and needed all the help he could get. When the account team members told him they couldn't assist, he felt disappointed and alienated. What happened? The negative mindset led them to not even try to open up any opportunities. In effect, by shutting down the CTO, they lost a lot of goodwill with their valuable contact.

Offensive Spirit Scenario—What Really Happened

After hearing the bad news about the CTO needing a deeper discount, the offensively minded team members used the most effective weapon in a salesperson's armory—the conditional tense. "Well, setting aside the discount situation, if we were to find a solution, what have you got in mind moving forward?" By saying this, they threw out a grain of hope by discussing what the CTO needed.

At this point, it got interesting. Team members learned about three major projects the company was having trouble funding. As the discussion continued, more details spilled out. They recognized a great deal of interesting business might be won if only the price were right.

Why was price so important? After all, the whole project was massive. Even a 10 percent discount would look quite small in the grand scheme. But it turned out that, although price was an issue, cash flow was the pressing problem. The CTO simply didn't have enough cash to pay for the equipment, given the usual terms and conditions offered.

By the end of the discussion, we had come to a number of solutions for several projects. We identified a need to justify a fairly stiff additional discount to our employer. We also offered to find a way to help alleviate a cash-flow problem. In the end, we did business at a reasonable level of discount, which was predicated by a tiered spending commitment. And we turned to a commercial bank to assist with the financing.

On our next visit, not only were we able to present a comprehensive solution for the CTO, but we also discovered an in-country skills shortage. That led to an opportunity to put together a turnkey solution for additional projects that would bring in more revenue.

Commentary

The offensively minded team members went into the meeting determined to succeed. They listened to the CTO's concerns. They didn't say no to anything. And they thought about solutions to the opportunities presented to them. Where they had reservations, they promised to look for workarounds. In general, they got onto the CTO's side of the table.

Their reward? The CTO opened up and told them his problems so they could offer solutions.

Now you might say if he'd done that in the first place, we could have helped him without all the fuss. But it simply doesn't work like that. You have to demonstrate both empathy and concern first. More importantly, you have to show a can-do attitude to problem solving.

It always takes aggression and this offensive spirit. Back at headquarters, no one thought giving the discount was a good idea, plus it was highly irregular to involve a bank on behalf of a customer. But team members showed the potential for success while securing the overall spend with tiered discounting and rebates. Then they acted as a go-between for the customer and the bank. By doing all this, the team got a yes when most people would have given up. They seized the initiative.

That's what having an offensive spirit can accomplish.

Real Life Example 2

I became engaged with an account team in one of the Arabian Gulf states, working with a local bank to secure substantial compute business in its data center. As is often true in emerging markets, customers' buying techniques can be somewhat immature; in this particular scenario, the CIO's team had bought into technology that wasn't well suited to their needs.

Specifically, the CIO wanted to buy more suitable hardware and software from the account team or their competitors. At the same time, he was hoping to sell the old equipment to the vendor and discount it from the price of the new gear.

Negative Scenario—What Could Have Happened

When this idea was raised, the account team responded well by telling the CIO it was indeed possible to buy back the equipment—that the account team could use online tools to estimate a price its company could pay for the gear. Even more impressive, the account team had an application on a mobile device that allowed it to do the number crunching.

Unfortunately, as always seems to happen in these situations, there turned out to be quite a significant delta (in the wrong direction) between the price the customer wanted for the used equipment and what the account team was authorized to give.

In this negative scenario, the account team became frustrated that, despite its ability to address the problem including its slick procedures to provide an instant quote, the customer was disappointed and dismissive. Again, bear in mind that the CIO was not a confidence trickster trying to hoodwink the account team out of its commission. On the contrary, he was an executive struggling with a complex problem—one that had been waking him up in the middle of the night for weeks. He was looking to the account team to find a solution.

Frustration mixed with disappointment is rarely a good combination. In this scenario, the inevitable happened, and the deal became difficult to close. Worse than that, the relationship was fatally damaged because the account team was viewed as ineffective. (Read more about this in the commentary section.)

Offensive Spirit Scenario—What Really Happened

In reality, having realized their own buy-back scheme wouldn't cut it, the account team started to talk to the CIO about what he'd do if something close to the price he was seeking for his secondhand equipment were approved. If they could sort out that problem, would he place his business with them (the conditional close)? His answer was an unequivocal yes.

This team, full of offensive spirit and confidence, left the CIO with little doubt they could fix the problem. Heed this warning: be careful to make sure the customer understands you have some work to do and decisions must be made before a final answer can be given; otherwise, you'll be in danger of setting misleading expectations.

Make Problem Solving Your Focus

At this point, it's always excellent to have a reason to call back, particularly at this high level. If you don't identify a pain point for the customer (and therefore an opportunity for you), a call in the future to say "Hi ... I'm just staying in touch" is ineffective. Salespeople frequently do this to me, and I find it tiresome.

But if you've been asked to fix something, then you've got a reason to call with an update or a final solution. And don't forget that an update is important. What you're doing about the situation and how much time you need to get to a conclusion is important information for someone with a problem, and your call will be appreciated. You're also continuing to build the relationship.

Let's get back to the story. The account manager had a friend in London who dealt in secondhand hardware. That friend was able to make a reasonable offer on the kit list that (nearly) met the CIO team's expectations. This was combined with an aggressive mix of discounting and blending of services that made it an excellent transaction for the customer. As a result, the account team successfully closed the deal.

Commentary

First, the offensive spirit of the team made this deal work. Lesser individuals would have left the conversation at the point when their online application identified the buy-back price. They'd assume that the CIO was only bluffing as part of the negotiation and that he'd been given the best price he could get, so he'd better get on board or miss the boat.

I don't know why this type of cynical and ultimately self-defeating attitude abounds among salespeople. Perhaps their constant exposure to the cut and thrust of the market makes them develop a shell of cynicism and suspicion.

The problem is that this attitude tends to lead people into assuming the worst of each other. Yet in reality, we're all in business to make money to support our families and do the best job we can for our customers, employers, and teammates. Customers aren't out there waking up every morning thinking about how they can turn over account teams. On the contrary, most executives do need a lot of help, and if approached in the right way, they provide opportunity for enterprising salespeople to present a plethora of solutions.

However, you won't be receiving calls any time soon from customers saying, "Please help me; I really need you." When they're in trouble, they tend to be defensive and behave in passive-aggressive ways. Your task is to break through the barriers, find out the issues, and strive to provide solutions.

Real Life Example 3

This example is one of my favorites. It relates to a higher-education institution in England, for which the account team I was working with had done a great job of building preference. The institution was on the verge of signing a large deal for telephone infrastructure.

The problem? The site for the system wasn't ready, but the budget had to be spent and the equipment had to be shipped before the institution's year-end. It sounds like a great situation for a salesperson, doesn't it? But in this scenario, the account team nearly made a mess of it.

Negative Scenario—What Could Have Happened

The account team wasn't much concerned about the deal. Team members believed it was in their pockets. They also believed year-end budget spend constraints were the customer's problem, so they did nothing to address it.

What's the anathema of offensive spirit? Complacency. It not only leaves the door open for competitors but also starts to damage the relationship with the customer. It's the old matter of the salesperson not empathizing with the customer's problems. This leads to accusations of arrogance from the client and possibly long-term resentment—not what you want.

Offensive Spirit Scenario—What Really Happened

Fortunately, the account manager started to think about this budget problem and stepped in to act in a positive, aggressive way. Her first reaction was to ask internally if her company could somehow keep the equipment warehoused and pass title to the customer. This wasn't acceptable for a number of accounting and legal reasons so, applying the GOYA principle, she found warehousing close to the customer's site and negotiated a price to hold all of the equipment for the additional three months required. She then went back to her company to negotiate the relatively minor discount required to pay for this. She then renegotiated with the customer's procurement department to get one purchase order for her company and another for the warehousing company.

The deal was closed, the customer got exactly what he wanted, the account team got an earlier order than they had expected, and (most important) the relationship was enhanced because the account team had solved the issue.

Commentary

It sounds as if the account manager was doing the customer's job for him, and that's true—she was. But it's absolutely amazing how often this happens. It's even more amazing how frequently account teams let the opportunity slip to step up and assist their customers.

Don't underestimate how difficult your customers find it to get things done. They may be facing inflexible administrators, strict rules, or even a lack of initiative. These barriers customers experience can become gifts to a forward-thinking salesperson. Incredibly, account teams often miss seeing them.

Conclusion on the Examples

Showing an offensive spirit carried the day in my three scenarios. If account teams are coached and motivated into saying "We will smash through every barrier until we close the deal," then they will naturally respond to the challenges the customer puts in their way, overcome them, and achieve solutions.

Offensive spirit addresses variable situations you can't plan for. It's your job as a leader to do what's required to ensure team members behave with tenacity, aggression, and creativity.

4 Concentration of Resources

Bang. Don't dribble!—**General Sir Martin Farndale**, *Commander First (British) Corps in 1986 (talking about how to deploy artillery in massive, concentrated barrages rather than in small, insignificant strikes)*

I think it's because we never really committed to the sport. So ... until about four or five years ago, we dabbled. And we're not good at dabbling. I think we're at our best when we commit.—**Mark Parker**, *CEO of Nike, on CNBC in June 2009 (talking about Nike's initially unsuccessful forays into the skateboarding market)*

For the military, concentration of resources is about throwing all of your might at a narrow front and smashing the enemy, its lines of communications, and its logistical tail. This can overcome numerical disadvantage and create momentum in attack.

From a sales perspective, concentrating on areas of likely success is vital. Many sales leaders organize teams on a geographical basis and give the teams a list of accounts that's often more extensive than they can realistically target. These leaders are more concerned about coverage than about focusing on areas of likely breakthrough and high levels of potential sales success. This topic can be controversial because coverage is important for most businesses—and if you're addressing SME clients, you do often need to find a way to cover millions of customers. However, this book isn't addressing that type of business model. Rather, it focuses on the high-touch, business-to-business sales environment in which you're more likely to be covering hundreds of accounts, not thousands.

Sales managers normally divide the total number of accounts they're given by the number of account managers and then distribute the

In General Schwarzkopf's famous "left hook" into Kuwait in 1991 during the first Gulf War, the allied armies completely outflanked the Iraqi Army. They were behind the Iraqis before they had any time to react, which preceded a complete route. Exploiting their technological advantage in terms of rapid maneuverability, the allied armies were able to overcome their numerical disadvantage. (Military doctrine normally assumes that attacking forces have to outnumber defenders by 3:1, and the allies were nowhere close to this ratio.)

The lesson? It's important to focus effort. By concentrating his forces to the west of the Iraqi positions in Kuwait, Schwarzkopf achieved numerical superiority in the locality of the attack and rolled through the defenders with little resistance. Careful planning and rapid execution combined with extraordinary logistics enabled the allied forces to get to their forming-up areas in Saudi Arabia. They went across the start line long before the Iraqis knew what was happening.

accounts equally—this is not an effective method. It's important to be more imaginative and concentrate resources in the areas most likely to bear fruit.

A junior account manager I spoke to recently had been given six hundred accounts to oversee! He told me he was struggling to cover them, and we discussed why. We computed the following:

Table 4.1
Insufficient Time Allocation When a Manager Has Too Many Accounts

Hours available per year (10 hours/day for 240 days)	2,400
Hours lost to nonselling activities	480
Selling hours available	1,920
Hours per customer per year (600 customers)	3 hours 12 minutes

And remember, that three hours per customer includes travel time. Clearly, this situation is total nonsense, but it's happening in companies all over the world. It's easy to say this account manager should be focusing on the most important accounts, but many salespeople don't think like that. He strives to cover all the bases, becomes completely unfocused, and spends far more time than is healthy with no-hope accounts. Much worse, potentially fruitful accounts that do need his time get little to no attention. Thus, opportunity is squandered.

Because your resources need to be concentrated on areas of maximum potential, you're better off working hard to segment accounts and deploy teams in the smartest way possible.

Segmenting Accounts to Achieve Concentration of Resources

The number of accounts a company has and how to segment them is often shown as a pyramid. The high-value large enterprises and public sector institutions are at the apex, the SMEs are at the base, and the mid-markets are logically sandwiched between them.

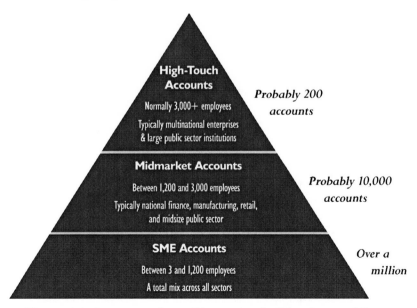

Figure 4.1. Segmentation of Accounts by Number and Type

Now, only you and the leadership team of your company can decide how to address this total market. Because we're primarily discussing the high-touch apex of this pyramid, let me concentrate my efforts there. But for the sake of completeness, I include likely go-to-market scenarios for each pyramid segment in the following table. (Channel partners refer to the organizations that take your products and services to market and have direct contact with the end customers—resellers, distributors, etc.)

Table 4.2

Accounts per Account Manager and Go-to-Market Scenarios

Account Type	Approximate # of Accounts per Manager	Go to Market
High Touch	10 maximum, but fewer as the accounts become strategic	A high concentration of resources is placed on these accounts with high-touch account management and a large focus on presales personnel and internal effort.
Midmarket	50	There's a much lower focus in terms of resources. Use of channel partners to provide more high-touch relationships is required. This is a tricky area in terms of finding balance between direct (your own resources deployed on accounts) and indirect (use of the channel).
SME	100s or even 1000s	By necessity, this segment needs to be covered by a well-organized and motivated channel network, which is outside the scope of this book.

High-Touch Selling

High-touch selling refers to concentrating resources in high-yielding accounts. It requires the account team to build close relationships throughout the organization, not only focusing on the CxOs but also properly covering and consulting middle-management teams as the engagement matures.

The following sections explain key areas common to all high-touch selling engagements.

Building Relationships

You've no doubt heard the adage "People buy people," which means individuals are inclined to buy products from people they like. But strong relationships don't come easily. Building rapport is extremely difficult with individuals who tend to be 250 percent overloaded in time available to complete their tasks.

When discussing offensive spirit, I mentioned that executives all have problems they need to solve. This provides opportunities for salespeople to build on their relationship with managers and executives. If salespeople can be seen as contributors or trusted advisors, not only will their relationship build, but they'll be called in the next time leaders have a problem to solve.

Becoming a Trusted Advisor

The term "trusted advisor" is one of the more hackneyed clichés in the sales vocabulary; nonetheless, becoming one is a desirable goal of a salesperson regarding contacts in an account. Arriving at this position takes a lot of skill. How do you get from having your suggestion to invest in a particular software regarded as a sales pitch to having the same suggestion regarded as a nugget of trusted advice?

Unfortunately, there's no simple answer. It's a matter of building trust over time. The salesperson has to be able to bring value to the account. Here, the advantage of focusing on the account becomes obvious. As the salesperson spends time wandering the corridors, attending meetings, and having informal conversations (the best way to build relationships and gain intelligence), opportunities to add value abound. People will need information, pricing, return-on-investment calculations, and documentation. A salesperson who can provide these necessities in a timely, friendly way rapidly becomes seen as a force for good and is on the way to being regarded as a trusted advisor.

Alternative to Trusted Advisor Doesn't Cut It

Take a minute to consider the alternative to this high-touch, trusted-advisor approach. Dashing from account to account, the account manager realistically doesn't have time to add value or build relationships. Inevitably, he or she is forced into finding out what deals are in the offing, making a bid, and hurtling off to the next account. Under these circumstances, this person will never be considered a trusted advisor.

In this section, I present examples of working toward being a trusted advisor by customers.

I worked with an account team in the United States that had built great relationships with the CIO's team in one of the mid-tier airlines. The team members had done commendable work providing information and advice on data centers, security, and contact centers. Although they hadn't closed the sale after nearly two quarters of effort, they'd built up a feeling of being trusted advisors with the CIO's team. In fact, they had such a good reputation with the IT department of the airline that it led them to obtain a meeting with the CIO—something deemed impossible before the team had been instructed to focus on the account.

Even more remarkably, they'd been in the CIO's office only a few moments when he told them he needed them to address his wide area network cost base because it was costing too much. He instructed his own team to work with the account team to come up with an answer. A tighter relationship between the teams ensued, and sales quickly followed.

This shows how building relationships based on trust creates a circle of strengthening bonds and ever-increasing sales.

In another case, I was highly impressed by a salesperson who was the lead account executive on a multinational bank in London, England. He had one of the closest trusted-advisor relationships I've ever experienced. Here's what amazed me most: when I asked the CIO exactly what he got from this salesperson, he told me the salesperson gave him trustworthy feedback on the bank's own products.

Let me explain. The bank was busy driving its international Internet-banking initiative, which involved a wide set of services for people with bank accounts in multiple countries and currencies. It just so happened the account executive was one of those people with money in several overseas accounts. What's more, many of his colleagues were in the same position. In the end, the account executive and his colleagues provided the CIO and, through him, the product managers at the bank with a focus group to test and improve the banking products.

As a result, the relationship between the teams was maintained at a high level. You won't be surprised to hear that their status as trusted advisors crossed over into the products the account team was selling. Thus, they broke sales records year after year based on this relationship.

Again, contrast this with a less focused approach in which account managers dart from customer to customer without the time or inclination to concentrate on providing meaningful value to their clients.

Building Internal Champions

Over the years, I've noticed that, in some strange way, those on the customer side who are working with salespeople like to be recognized for the effort they're putting into the relationship. This isn't about an occasional free lunch, football game, or round of golf—much as these are welcome perks of business life. People like to be recognized for the efforts they expend with a sales team because, surprisingly, it gives them a certain amount of status in their own organizations.

A lot of salespeople overlook this important bit of psychology. Because they're so used to being beaten up by their customers, they assume they're viewed as enemies as opposed to vehicles for their contacts to achieve enhanced status inside their own organizations. Savvy salespeople see this as an opening and make sure they take advantage of it in the relationship-building effort.

The following examples provide insight into how to create your own champions inside client companies.

Use Your Champion to Deliver Your Proactive Advice

Once the sales team has built a degree of trust, it's important to circulate the feel-good factor around the customer organization. This is where the champion comes in. A good salesperson will make sure that every piece of advice, warning, or suggestion is channeled to the customer via a designated company champion. It brings these key advantages:

- People within the company are far more likely to believe and rely on internal players than salespeople from a partner or vendor. It's not because salespeople are deemed dirty or dishonest; it's because people perceive colleagues to know the company and have its best interests at heart.

- You can greatly boost the internal status of your champions with their peers and bosses by providing them with a wide range of ideas and new information. This will help their careers, compensation, and self-esteem. It also allows the sales team to build a stronger relationship and provides a reliable conduit into the customer organization—a win-win set of circumstances.

The following examples illustrate this principle in action.

Product Websites

A sales team in Belgium was working with a major multinational fast-moving consumer goods manufacturer. These days, companies like this have websites for their major products—in this case, a fabric softener. Performance on these websites is important, yet the client was inadvertently allowing response times on the site to elongate because of what turned out to be network overloading.

The assigned salesperson had the benefit of concentrating on this account on an international basis. Because of this, she knew that not only was website performance an important matrix for gauging IT and marketing performance, but it was proving difficult to measure. The company in question had hundreds of brand websites. It had become reduced to tasking teams of people with testing performance by logging onto the websites on a rotational basis to measure the time the squeeze page took to load. Given the vagaries of network loading and website use, this approach was inefficient and, ultimately, didn't work. Consequently, the company couldn't guarantee how long a webpage would take to load at any given time.

The account team engaged a new professional services team that had developed a set of noninvasive probing tools. Team members could look at a sample of a customer's websites and see what they could discover. They found that the response times were, at their worst, forty seconds compared with the optimum of four seconds. This automated process was far more accurate than the roomful-of-geeks approach (putting it bluntly) that the customer had been using. The results were then used to determine where the problem lay. In this case, the difficulty was a networking fault inside the customer's data center.

Until this point, the customer hadn't been involved; rather, the discovery was an act of stealth presales. Next, the salesperson approached her champion on the CIO's team and presented the results. She suggested he might position this piece of analysis as work he had asked the salesperson's company to perform free of charge because he had suspected this may have been the problem all along.

Rather than regarding this as sneaky, it was a clever bit of positioning that helped the champion further his reputation (and career, compensation, and self-esteem). More importantly, it gave the company in question a clear indication of what was causing the problem. And finally, the salesperson was able to sell a solution that not only rectified the problem but also positioned and closed a deal while using her professional services team to monitor the entire suite of global websites against a set of jointly developed matrices.

In this case, the account team found the right amount of focus to spend time on the account, develop relationships with potential champions, and get a chance to deeply understand the business problems the company faced. As with most successful salespeople, this account manager was an amateur psychologist as well as an empathetic salesperson. With her combined skills, she identified a champion who was ambitious and wanted to contribute and succeed. She then matched him with a business problem that needed a solution.

Had the account manager had gone straight to the CIO's office and said, "Your websites are performing badly, and we have a solution to fix them," it's highly unlikely she would have succeeded. An internal champion had a far better chance of bringing in the sale.

Unsupported Dealer Room

In a second example, let me relate an interesting scenario that played out in the dealing room of a major international bank. Once again, the account team—particularly the account manager—was intensely focused on this account on a global basis. As the engagement matured, the presales engineering team suspected that many of the devices in the dealer room had unmatched software loads, which would have led to major functionality, reliability, and security issues.

Unsurprisingly, you can't wander into a dealer room like this (where billions of dollars are traded every day) with a screwdriver and soldering iron and ask if you can take a look. Thus, it was difficult for the sales engineer and account manager to prove their suspicions. They pulled together as much collateral information as they could in terms of equipment sold, the versions of the software supplied with each device, and possible problems if all these devices still had their original software loads.

This is where their company champion came in. The account team advised this individual of the potential issues and recommended that a full diagnostic check be run to pinpoint and verify the issues. This would involve down times and a lot of programmatic work to ensure the tests were run properly. Once again, the CIO would have rejected this exercise out of hand had it come from the vendor account team, but because it was introduced via the internal champion, the account team managed to get the diagnostic program organized.

After the tests had been run, the team discovered that the sales engineer's suspicions had been correct, and a great deal of rectification work and new equipment was required. This excellent piece of selling was accomplished in a covert way that made it painless for the customer and allowed the champion to position the whole effort as his pet project.

As an interesting paradox, the CIO mildly rebuked the account manager at the end of the process. "Shouldn't you people have alerted us to this problem rather than allowing us to discover it ourselves?" he asked. The account manager was acute enough to say that yes, indeed, the account team was at fault and that he would ensure it was more proactive in the future!

Nobody said making sales was easy, but if you can achieve the required results, then you have to absorb a bit of pain en route. Regard it as a character-building opportunity.

Boosting the Profile of Your Champion

You'll find it's quite useful to build the champion's credibility as the person within the organization who knows all about your products and services—the go-to individual when it comes to any issues with your company. What can you do to enhance the reputation of your champion? Let me share the following techniques, which have been used success- fully.

First, invite the champion to meet executives from your own organi- zation whenever possible. This is always tricky because executives want to meet their peers, not a middle manager, which your champion will almost certainly be. Be smart here and perhaps grab one of your execu- tives; then introduce the executive to your champion at an event, con- ference, sales meeting, exhibition, or lunch. In my experience, you'll have to lead the ensuing conversation proactively to avoid the awkward silences that often follow this type of introduction.

"This is Alan Jones from Acme, Inc., who's been working really hard with us for over a year to finish Acme's big fiber project. He's been a significant advocate for us."

This should be enough to get started, but make sure you're there to keep the conversation moving. It can be effective to prearrange that your champion introduce a topic you're struggling with internally. For example, if you are short of engineering resources in the account, your champion might mention to your executive that he'd like to see addi- tional engineers support a project that's coming to fruition in the near future. This can give you internal momentum to get things done and, of course, gives the customers additional horsepower to meet their objec- tives.

Bear in mind that this can work in both directions. Soon you'll find your champion reciprocating by introducing you to executives. This proves that the champion does indeed have access at a high level and is also well connected with your company.

As your champion develops a relationship at the top of your company, encourage this person to stay in touch through LinkedIn or an occasional e-mail, for example. When executives from the two companies meet, you can invite him or her in as an observer and provider of shop-floor information.

Another technique is to invite the champion to your customer events as a guest speaker to talk about successful engagement and case studies with your company. Although not everyone enjoys public speaking, most people are pleased to be invited and will recognize it as a chance to establish professional credibility with an audience outside of their own company. As a by-product, the champion's internal credibility will be boosted by the invitation to be a key participant in your event.

When you have good news about cash rebates, new products, and price decreases, let your champion know first, and make sure that he or she passes the news on to management and peers. You need to continually associate this person in a positive way with your company. The unfortunate corollary is that you need to deliver the bad news when it comes—and you know it will. This may include price hikes, essential product end-of-life action, or changes to rebate policy—all of these can increase the pain of your day. Under no circumstance should you let people in the customer organization hear any of this kind of information from your champion. Simply communicate it clearly and position it in a gentle way that minimizes any psychological impact. Your champion won't do this as well as a salesperson, plus you don't want to tarnish his carefully burnished image with negative news.

How Do You Recognize Potential Champions?

Four key characteristics distinguish all successful internal champions. The salesperson can unleash his or her inner psychologist to identify these individuals and groom them. These characteristics include the following:

- **Ambitiousness**—Standout individuals in most companies clearly want to get things done, drive progress, and make a name for themselves in the bargain. They're energetic, optimistic, and knowledgeable about their company and its products, services, and processes. These individuals want to be seen as achievers. They're frequently frustrated about the lack of recognition they receive for their hard work and about the difficulty of obtaining opportunities to climb the greasy corporate pole.

- **Openness**—Many customers are suspicious of salespeople. Perhaps we all have that bias buried somewhere in our psyches. This impression impedes a salesperson's progress inside client organizations. Breaking down protective barriers can be hard work, and people with this bias are unlikely to ever make good champions, even with the best will in the world. The antithesis of this type of person is the bright and open individual who genuinely enjoys working with third-party companies. This person wants to build relationships and can see instinctively how this type of relationship can enhance his or her career.

- **Eagerness to Learn**—People who demonstrate the characteristics just described will also be naturally inquisitive. They'll want to find out more about your products and services, not only in the context of how these can help their companies but also as a way of enhancing their professional qualifications. This hunger for knowledge can easily be sated by providing materials and training. Never underestimate the power of assisting others with self-improvement.

- **Egotism**—It naturally follows that people with solid confidence are well suited to be champions. They'll be looking to boost their reputation and image within their organizations, and if they can find a way of doing that through association with your company, they almost certainly will.

In conclusion, you're looking for a person who's enthusiastic about entering into a symbiotic relationship that will benefit both of you while providing access to those higher up in the target company.

Strategic Accounts

The ultimate in concentration of resources consists of establishing strategic accounts. For your company to be successful, these customers require extreme focus. When selecting the accounts, several factors come into play.

The customer will be a large player in your market and typically in the Fortune 100 or local equivalent. In emerging markets, strategic customers will often be from key national industries (e.g., oil, gas, and petrochemicals in the Middle East; gold and diamonds in Africa; and iron ore, oil, and timber in Latin America).

Typically, your company will have established a strong presence in the account, which you will need to maintain and grow—a matter of applying focus to build out from a strong beachhead.

Alternatively, you may wish to create strategic accounts where your company's presence is somewhat weak. For historical reasons, it can happen that you simply haven't penetrated an account to the degree you would expect. If so, using the strategic account approach may make sense. A word of warning, however—just because you think you should be present in an account doesn't mean you can be successful. Make sure you carefully qualify before you start throwing resources at a lost cause. At the beginning of this chapter, we discussed the military amassing forces at an enemy's weak point to achieve superiority and breakthrough. If one of your competitors is so firmly ensconced in a potential target company that you'd need a massive effort to make any progress, it may be prudent to look for lower hanging fruit. This isn't being negative; it's simply recognizing that every organization has finite resources. You need to deploy your resources with care—that is, in places where you have a good chance of winning.

Following is a decision matrix to copy based on an IT thread of examples. It will help you select the right accounts for strategic status.

Table 4.3

Decision Matrix for Selecting Strategic Accounts

Factor	Comment
Total Customer Revenue	Look at the trend over three to five years. Is revenue growing, indicating expansion?
Profit	Again look at the trend over three to five years. Increasing profits indicate potential for sales. If profits are shrinking, though, check to see if there's an insertion opportunity that would help the company cut costs and grow shrinking profits.
IT Spend	It's surprisingly easy to gain intelligence from the market about past and upcoming budgets if your salespeople are talking to the customer and other suppliers to build up the picture. IT spend is an important number. An upward trend indicates buoyancy in the account.
Number of Employees	This number is easy to obtain from annual reports, etc. It clearly indicates scale and, therefore, potential for sales.
Number of Sites	For many classes of company—telecoms, networks, cloud compute, mobility, and so on—this is an important indicator for potential business because driving a collaborative environment generates a lot of spend.
Strength of Competition in Account	Good intelligence can indicate the level of spend with each of your competitors. Typically, look for fragmented spending with multiple competitors. If you see concentrated spending with one competitor, qualify carefully. That said, also be aware that sometimes strong opportunities for insertion exist because the customer feels trapped in a monogamous relationship with one partner.
Size of Sales for Your Company	Has this been a successful account in previous years? Is there a strong growth trend? How could this be further enhanced by expansion into new areas?

Size of Future Opportunity for Your Company	Typically consider the coming three years. The need for accurate intelligence is paramount. Beware of optimism based on the input of business-development people who say things like, "This is a huge customer so we must have masses of opportunity." Qualification is king here rather than reliance on unfounded speculation. At the same time, look at previous numbers to ensure you're pushing your future estimates aggressively based on growth and expansion possibilities.
Are Resources Available to Address the Account in a Focused Manner?	This is a crucial factor. It's no use starting down a strategic account path if you don't staff your efforts sufficiently because the whole concept will wither on the vine. Make sure you have resources to cover the account properly.

Superior Focus

Once you've decided on your strategic accounts, build a team around them. As stated in the foregoing table, it's critical to have enough people with the requisite amount of talent to do the job. At minimum, you'll need to appoint a top salesperson (strategic account director) and two presales technical people.

Assign the team members solely to the account in question, and ensure they will live and breathe it for the foreseeable future. This dedication is the ultimate expression of the concentration of resources discussed throughout this chapter.

The team members have a big responsibility to build a deep relationship with both executives and middle management in the target account. The job is not easy, and I'm often asked what makes an ideal strategic account director. With this question in mind, I've tabulated a checklist of the qualities I've noticed in successful individuals occupying these roles.

Table 4.4

Qualities of a Successful Strategic Account Director

Quality	Comment
Track Record	As in all staff selection matters, past performance is usually a good indicator of future delivery. If that track record is in the same or a similar account, it's a clear signal of likely success. Be careful, though, as many a salesperson comes off an excellent run in one environment and is completely out of his or her depth in another.
Relationships in Account	Recruiting a salesperson who already has relationships in the target account is well and good. Ideally, this person will have been working the account on your behalf rather than a competitor's. It's confusing and slightly surreal for the customer and awkward at best for the salesperson to suddenly switch loyalties. It can work, but in my view, it's a risk. It's tough to be pushing a competitive value proposition one day and then turn up the next with a completely different pitch for another company.
Ability to Build Strong Relationships	If you don't have an internal candidate who's already well underway in terms of account relationships, then look for internal and external candidates who've shown an ability to build strong links with similar accounts in terms of size and industry. If they've done it once, they can do it again. If you're convinced the candidate does have relationship-building mojo, there's a good chance of success moving forward.
Inside Own Company Relationships	Here's an excellent reason to use internal candidates. Great salespeople know how to corral internal resources and get things done. I often view these individuals as the customer's champion inside the salesperson's own organization. It's about working to build deals, getting product changes made, expediting orders, adjusting standard contracts, and negotiating payment terms. These incredibly valuable issues for the customer make the salesperson a key partner for the business. It's difficult to come into a new company and have the type of relationships and street savvy to carry this off. Most people need a minimum of six months to make the necessary internal connections. During those six months, the customers may well feel they're not getting the anticipated value they wanted from the strategic account director. Although I don't discount the idea of outsiders coming in to become strategic account directors, I think it can be highly challenging.

Quality	Comment
Intelligence	You're looking for someone who will be bright, hungry for knowledge, and able to process all of the discovered facts into a big picture. As part of this, problem-solving skills will be required to navigate through complexities with multiple moving parts and dependencies. Large accounts generate big challenges, and the strategic director will need a sharp mind to navigate through the morass.
Inquisitive	The key component of selling is discovery. By talking to people and asking questions, you build up a landscape of what's going on and how you, as a salesperson, can structure your efforts to benefit the customer. An inquiring mind is necessary to the role of strategic account director. Otherwise, the chances of building an excellent pipeline of sales are slim.
Innovative	Complex problems need innovative solutions. Big accounts are always looking for great new ideas to create competitive advantage or cut costs (ideally both). An innovative strategic account director adds considerable value to the client company. The customers themselves rarely acknowledge this, but all the great account managers I've worked with have provided a stream of helpful ideas to their customers.
Ability to Write Well	This one may come as a surprise for employers of generation Z candidates. Many people assume that anyone born after 1980 doesn't read books, writes in stylized SMS speak, and can barely string a coherent sentence together. This generation communicates through social media in a way that older people have no way of logically interpreting. Sorry, but you can't disseminate a complex problem and derive a satisfactory solution on Twitter. You need to produce documents, spreadsheets, and presentations that describe problems and solutions in a way that large numbers of stakeholders understand and can act on. I doubt this will ever change. Good writing is a critical skill in the strategic account director's toolbox.

Quality	Comment
Ability to Present Well	The most impactful messaging is delivered face-to-face in presentations. When we see someone delivering slides every week, mostly we experience extremely poor execution. People read off slides, crowded with information, and provide little structure to their messaging—a terrible waste of an opportunity to communicate. I hate to see a painstakingly arranged meeting of decision makers lose interest after the first slide. They fish out their smartphones, start looking at their cuff links and watches, and generally turn off the message. You absolutely need to get people into strategic accounts who can perform using this critical method of communication. I never employ people in these roles without giving them a presentation task and critically appraising their capabilities.
Customer Industry Knowledge	Every industry has a complex set of vocabulary and norms that provides the currency for everyday discussions. If your candidates can't understand and participate in these discussions, they are off to a dismal start. But there's more to it. If they have a deep understanding of the industry in question, then they're more likely to absorb information about the customer and be able to innovate effectively. However, I've noticed that most great salespeople can absorb industry knowledge and taxonomy extremely quickly, so be careful not to immediately reject otherwise strong candidates because they're industry outsiders.
Own Industry Knowledge	This is important in terms of choosing a candidate for a critical strategic account role. To become a trusted advisor in an account, in 90 percent of customer environments, account managers will need to be experts in all matters relating to the industry. The focus of the customer CxO team will always be on their own core activities, and the products and services will only be contextual. It's the salesperson's job to ensure that the company's offerings are understood and perceived to provide competitive advantage. The salesperson has to explain trends in the industry and ensure they're reflected in upcoming plans plus present well-thought-out opinions and advice to members of the CxO suite and those below that level.

If you can recruit, nurture, and retain sales personnel who fit the majority of these criteria, then you're well on the way to securing individuals who can become trusted advisors at high levels of the customer hierarchy.

There may still be a tendency to see strategic account sales personnel as primarily socialites who play golf, attend sporting events, and consume gourmet food and alcohol with alarming frequency. Please don't kid yourself; this is an old-fashioned concept. Customers rarely have time for such luxuries in the modern business environment. They're far more interested in finding solutions to their problems and gaining competitive advantage than in burning time on corporate entertainment. That's not to say occasional lunches and playing eighteen holes of golf don't have their place, but they're not core to strategic account management.

Governance Structure

As your teams focus on strategic accounts, it will become important for you to manage progress in a new way. Running forecast calls and account reviews as well as making individual performance assessments will be part of your business-as-usual processes. Typically outside of your customers' knowledge, these are internally focused and address questions like "How are we doing against the target?"

Concentration of resources on important accounts opens up an opportunity to interact with customers in a new way by creating a governance structure.

I've seen this done successfully in a number of accounts all over the world, and in every case, it involves inviting key customer executives into a regular discussion with senior members of your own company. To add gravitas to the concept, I like to describe the group as the governance board. The level of participation depends on things such as the criticality of your products and services to the customer's business, the level of spend the customer has with you, and the comparative sizes of your companies.

In a large business-to-business engagement, I aim for VP involvement on both sides. The idea is for this board to meet at least once a quarter. From a sales perspective, you'd likely prefer once a month, but most busy executives will balk at that.

Typically, I'd expect to see the account team produce a document that enunciates who is on the board, the frequency of meetings, and the objectives of setting up the structure. Following are the initiatives usually included:

- Update the executives of the customer company on existing projects.

- Resolve technical and commercial issues.

- Present new technologies and ideas to the customer.

- Allow the customer to discuss key upcoming issues and requirements in the business.

Other objectives will be added, depending on the type of businesses involved. Often, customer executives are interested in how connections with your company can help them boost their own sales through joint marketing, sales engagement, and cobranding. Be sure to look for those opportunities and include them in the convening document to make it attractive to the customer.

Keep in mind that the customer won't want to do this at the outset. It will be just another call on executives' time and another way for a vendor to pitch on a regular basis. That means providing a compelling reason to make it worthwhile, and this is where selling skills come to the fore. I suggest finding a significant pain point and competitive advantage that the governance board can address. Then you'll get some traction.

The following compelling issues are examples of topics I've used to get customers' buy-in to the governance process. I also indicate how the subsequent engagement resulted in a payoff.

- Cybersecurity had become a significant worry for customers involved in online gaming. It was out of the hands of the IT team and on the desk of the CEO. The company I was working with had deep expertise in this area, and it made complete sense for executives from both sides to discuss the topic on a regular basis. In the end, a joint team was formed not only to bring engineering support to the customer (the account team was doing a good job of this) but also to devote R & D resources to solving the customer's unique problems. Before long, sales in this account soared because the relationship became so tight that supply of products and services ceased to be competitive. Rather, it became a matter for negotiation at board level.

- A public sector customer had been given challenging objectives for a national network rollout over five years and had issues with resources, expertise, and cash flow. The customer's first instinct was to treat potential vendors as enemies, but the account team smartly positioned a governance board that would address the issues holistically. Having signed up to this, the customer executives found they were able to access solutions for technology, skilled manpower shortages, and financing because they were engaging at a high level with their supplier, which they soon referred to as a partner.

One of the major payoffs of the governance process is that executives from both companies build relationships among themselves that add tremendous value to the management of the account. While the executives will probably communicate independently, the account team has the capability to manage some of the messaging to the customer. In the process, the team gets valuable insights coming in the opposite direction.

Here's a good example of this working well. A Middle Eastern company had confidential plans to relocate all of its contact centers to a consolidated location. The account team working on the company hadn't heard about this move, but as a result of CxO contact, details of the initiative and consequent technology upgrades were discussed at a business dinner. The account team was briefed by its executive and took a technology roadmap directly to the customer's CEO. The deal was engineered in the account team's favor before the competition even knew the company had new technology requirements.

From a customer perspective, this type of high-level contact brings a lot of advantages. Customers get to talk to suppliers at a senior level, but more importantly, because of the gradual buildup of trust resulting from the governance process, they confide in them and seek meaningful advice on mission-critical and career-affecting decisions. I can't overemphasize these benefits.

The unstoppable rise of procurement departments with their voracious appetite to commoditize everything has led to discomfort for customers. Procurement may lead to the purchasing of goods and services at the lowest prices, but this doesn't mean the resulting solutions are the best available. While I salute what procurement departments do, trust and personal contact are important parts of business that are being eroded by the modern trend of lowest-common-denominator purchasing. Building board-level relationships reverses the trend.

What Does a Governance Board Look Like?

The governance board should be built at two levels: a working team that meets about twice a month and an executive team that meets quarterly. It's important to coordinate scheduling of the meetings so the working team can gather and provide data for the executive board.

Working team—Although this team will vary from account to account, make sure you include a collection of cross-functional leaders who can make things happen on both sides of the table. Rather than specify exact structures, I provide the following chart of functional areas you're likely to discuss and will want to staff accordingly.

Table 4.5

Profile of a Working Team on a Governance Board

Functional Area	Your Company	Customer
Heads of Team	This strategic account director runs the meeting in co-operation with the customer opposite.	Usually your customer champion, this person cochairs the meetings with your strategic account director and drives all the content and contribution coming from the customer side.
Sales to the Customer	This is probably the strategic account director again who will cover upcoming projects, pricing, finance, etc.	This person is most likely a senior project manager from the customer side who will typically be supported by procurement executives.

Functional Area	Your Company	Customer
Purchases from the Customer	This is someone from procurement or other relevant department (IT, manufacturing, etc., depending on the customer's products and services). Purchasing from the customer is often overlooked in building a relationship. It's surprising how much goodwill and leverage you can generate by ensuring the customer has a vested interest from a revenue and profit perspective of building strong ties with your company.	This typically involves the sales team from the customer, although paradoxically this can be handled successfully by customer procurement executives. This sometimes happens because customer representatives strongly link what their company is buying from you with what your company wants to buy from them. Caution: avoid any type of reciprocal trading in these engagements, which is illegal in most markets. In this context, it becomes a question of ensuring the relationship is allowed to build in a 360-degree manner.
Sales with the Customer	In many instances, your customer may well be acting as a channel for your goods and services or vice versa. In the first instance, the customer is your channel to market so you need someone from your channel organization. In the second instance, you need someone from your sales organization who has an overview of customer sales via your company to third parties.	For a lot of customers, this is a critical part of the relationship, so someone at sales-director level should attend the working team meetings. The group tracks sales and discusses deals.
Marketing and Public Relations	This senior marketing person attends the meetings to discuss joint marketing funds, cobranding, press releases, and so on.	This is a customer's opposite number who can coordinate marketing and public relations issues.

Functional Area	Your Company	Customer
Supply Chain	In fruitful relationships, supply-chain issues are inevitably discussed, so a senior executive from customer services is a key member of the team to address important issues such as delivery, support, financing, and ongoing maintenance.	This is typically addressed from a customer perspective by senior project management personnel.
Quality	While this may be handled in supply-chain discussions, normally with high-technology hardware and software, strategic issues involving quality problems arise—mostly in software bug fixes. Quality assurance and development representatives may be required to attend meetings.	From a customer perspective, engineering and quality staff are involved.

This may seem horrendous to you: an enormous fight twice a month in which you struggle to control a bunch of whining customer middle managers. Often, they're never satisfied and want to use the governance process as a platform for complaining on a frequent basis.

But please don't despair. It *does* work if it's properly planned, chaired, and executed by the team leaders—your strategic account director and the customer champion. These leaders need to choose attendees carefully and not invite all of the people all of the time because it's seldom necessary. They set the agenda to address key issues and scrupulously create minutes and action lists as well as follow up on these with rigor. Nothing destroys the validity of regular meetings more than an inability to demonstrate valuable progress consistently. Therefore, the strategic account manager must hustle during and between meetings to make sure actions are generated and executed in a timely manner.

Executive team—I strongly recommend the executive team be composed of primarily CxOs. Although team composition varies from account to account, you'll want to field either a sales or geographic senior vice president and persuade the customer to nominate the CIO or COO for this role. Deputies will support them as necessary, and the other key attendees will be the strategic account director and customer champion. The board will be augmented by experts from the working team as necessary.

Key functions of the executive team consist of the following:

- **Set strategy**—We saw from the 360-degree nature of the working team that the board can address multiple aspects of a relationship with a customer. It's unlikely all of them will be appropriate, but the team properly addresses areas of synergy with clear strategic vision and direction.

- **Set objectives**—As with every strategy strand, the team sets SMART objectives that can be measured.

- **Monitor progress**—The executive team jointly gauges success, modifies execution techniques, and adjusts the original objectives as necessary.

- **Resolve disputes**—You needn't have been in business long to know that two departments, let alone two companies, working together usually have a range of disputes to resolve. The beauty of the executive team is this: First, it has the authority to sort things out. Second, because team members are at least one step removed from the problem, they're much less emotional about it and can be rational in resolving it. The positive spinoff? Nothing cements relationships better than joint problem resolution. These opportunities to work together pay off well as the partnership at board level matures.

Measurement Matrices—Lagging Factors

To measure success, a collection of matrices is needed to enable you to track progress. Again, these vary from account to account, but I'll share a few generically indicative factors I've seen used in many accounts. Keep in mind that these are *lagging* factors (i.e., they indicate what *has* happened as opposed to what is likely to happen in the future). (Later in this chapter is a balancing set of techniques that provide more predictive matrices.)

Table 4.6

Lagging Factors Used to Track Progress

Matrix	Your Perspective	Customer Perspective
Measurement of Sales to the Customer	Typically, this serves as your key measurement of how the relationship is performing.	The customer doesn't care about this unless the company has something important to gain. Normally, it's tied into a revenue agreement whereby the customer receives tiered discounts and rebates based on spend with you.
Measurement of Customer Sales to You	This is obviously not always appropriate. The account team doesn't get excited about it, but it's an important matrix for the customer.	This is a critical spinoff from doing business with you and needs to be monitored carefully. If it's going badly, the teams need to address it together. Your strategic account manager may end up spending time working as the customer's champion in your own organization.
Measurement of Customer Sales Via Your Company as a Channel	This is highly useful when appropriate. It's a classic win-win, with both companies benefiting from incremental profit and revenue.	The customer sees great benefit in this and views it as an excellent payoff from the relationship.
Measurement of Your Sales Using the Customer as a Channel	Again, this win-win scenario benefits both sides.	With hard work and careful positioning, not only can this enhance numbers but, ideally, the customer perceives it as a significant enhancement of the customer's value proposition to the market.

Measurement of Supply Chain Efficiency	This varies from account to account but typically is about improved delivery times, local stock holdings, time to provide spare parts, and so forth.	Improvements in these areas are always important for the customer. The company can lower costs by having smaller stock or spares holdings, deliver to customers more quickly to allow more rapid invoicing, meet customer deadlines efficiently, and get service support quickly and cost-effectively.
Quality Improvement	You instinctively know that improved quality leads to enhanced sales. This may be lower levels of faulty equipment, numbers of bugs identified, numbers of bugs fixed, etc.	Customers are always concerned about quality. Rarely does an executive team fail to aim for improved quality.

Score Cards—Leading Indicators

You may wish to take these matrices a step further and build a complete balanced scorecard system. One can fall into a trap of looking only at lagging indicators—what has already happened. A more balanced approach looks at leading indicators to act as performance drivers.

The four generic areas used as a framework for balanced scorecards include the following:

- Learning and growth

- Customer

- Business process

- Financial

Let's look at leading indicators in each of these areas. Use the following measurements (indicators) and apply them to specific strategic accounts.

Table 4.7

Leading Indicators in Four Areas that Aid Success

Area	Leading Indicator	Comments
Learning and Growth	Number of trained personnel to address specific customer issues	The more people you have who are properly prepared to work on your customer, the better your lagging indicators will look.
	Number of people properly briefed on the strategic plan	People can only execute against a plan if they're properly briefed. Success against the plan can be secured by maximizing this indicator.
	Number of people with an understanding of the customer's requirements	This requires you to properly capture and promulgate the customer's needs and then properly brief people on those needs.
	Appointment of mentors and tutors to ensure execution	It will often be possible to have personnel consulting with the main team to provide experience, expertise, and mentorship. This can be a deliberate and systemic process used as a leading indicator.
Business Process	Tools in place to properly manage the relationship	You need to plan tools for sharing information between the customer and the various functions of the company. These could be access to supply-chain data, numbers, bug fixes, etc.
	Performance matrices in place	This is a way of measuring with a *leading* indicator how well set up you are to measure *lagging* indicators. These mechanisms ensure you can capture and present business information accurately and in a timely fashion.

Area	Leading Indicator	Comments
Customer	Customer objectives clearly stated and articulated	Keeping the focus on what the customer wants ensures the relationship matures and prospers. You need to regularly review progress with customer objectives.
	Access to customer data and tools	Where appropriate, you need to know how the customer is performing against the customer's own chosen matrices, which the customer typically needs to provide. This foundation is a key leading indicator of future performance.
Financial	Ensure SMART objectives are set for both revenue and profit	By setting up and promulgating this information, you provide a clear leading indicator of upcoming success. It doesn't guarantee performance, of course, but not doing it almost certainly guarantees failure.

Executive Sponsorship

The final piece is to secure a top senior executive to sponsor the whole relationship. While you probably have an Senior Vice President on your executive team, aim for a CxO to be your executive sponsor. Ambitious account teams will look for CEO involvement, but COOs, CTOs, and CIOs are the more usual candidates.

This involvement brings clout to any engagement. Although it's unlikely you'll have more than one meeting a year between your executive and the customer executive, it brings psychological benefits in terms of perceived commitment and interest from your side as far as the customer is concerned. If push comes to shove, it also gives you the chance to engage the biggest of big hitters to get what's needed for the sake of your customer.

Strategic Account Case Study

As often happens, this successful engagement was born out of crisis. The sales organization was a multinational network company and the customer a giant telco. I chose this example because the telco had multiple requirements of the selling company, making it a multifaceted and therefore comprehensive example. In addition, in nearly every area, severe issues existed, resulting in customer dissatisfaction:

- The telco bought equipment to build their own networks and provide services to their customers. This massive set of platforms generated a lot of revenue and profit for the sales company. Needless to say, the telco felt it was paying too much and not receiving the financial benefits it deserved from its loyalty.

- The telco resold network equipment to their B2B customers. This was a competitive business with multiple channel partners fighting for market share. The telco leaders didn't feel the sales company was supporting them enough to maximize their penetration in the market.

- The sales company took the customer's connectivity products and bundled them with its own equipment to sell to its channel and subsequently to its end users. The telco leaders didn't think the sales company's people did this with sufficient enthusiasm or in a way that had a major impact on the telco's sales.

- Quality in the telco network was of paramount importance. Unfortunately, because the telco was working at the limits of the equipment's performance envelope, bugs arose. The telco not only found this unacceptable but was troubled by the length of time it took for the sales company to implement the fixes.

- Supply-chain issues, particularly delivery times and spares holdings, were critical for the customer's internal projects and also to meet the expectations of third-party B2B customers. Manufacturing snafus, high demand, and even customs-clearance issues had elongated delivery times and, worse still, had resulted in unpredictability. This caused great customer dissatisfaction.

- Cobranding, combined sales-force incentives, and joint messaging were critical to marketing. The telco was looking for major spinoffs in this area, and none had been forthcoming.

- The customer was keen to sell telco products, such as international connectivity and telephony, to the sales company. Telco leaders felt they weren't getting a reasonable share of wallet in this area. They didn't like the idea that their purchases were high but their sales of core product were not.

Execution of a Strategic Account Engagement

The situation had become so fouled up in the account that the sales company had to take drastic measures. It put together a multidisciplinary team to build a plan that would address the issues and form the basis of a document that could be shared with the customer.

The sales company addressed the issues as follows:

- **Network Sales to the Telco**—The company introduced a new scheme to track the spending of the telco and to give it tiered levels of discount as its spending increased and cash rebates as incremental targets were reached. (The advantages for the telco were obvious, but the supplier also benefited. The process involved communication with the customer that revealed important insights into the customer's spending plans, project requirements, and general approach to the market. This kind of intelligence is vitally important to the salesperson. It creates the type of customer intimacy that's difficult to generate in an ordinary engagement.)

- **Resale of equipment**—A major effort resulted in a joint sales engagement to drive the telco's efforts in the market. The companies created joint sales teams that would share intelligence on target customers, plan sales campaigns, and call on the customer together. They would establish joint sales targets and closely coordinate the overall effort. The telco was keen to break into this market, so this move provided the company with a lot of value. It's crucial to remember what pushes the customer's hot buttons. In this case, the sales company already had a big channel to market and didn't need the telco as an additional route to its customers; on the contrary, the introduction of a strong new player caused a bit of disruption. The board had to judge whether the move made sense or not in terms of value—just another example of the constant compromises business people have to make. In this case, it paid off.

- **Construction of new joint market offerings**—This joint venture proved to be a successful way of innovating in the market. By concentrating a team of strong technical experts from both sides in a hothouse environment, the companies were able to innovate to create a number of key products. They used the telco's connectivity and service offering combined with the sales company's technology. Their success in the market was substantial: new hosted Internet protocol telephony solutions, broadband-based "office-in-a-box" products, and cloud-based security offerings all followed.

- **Quality improvement**—A serious focus on quality was brought to bear. The board embraced the idea of executive sponsorship, and the executive vice president responsible for research and development was appointed to provide focus on the problems the customer was experiencing. Regular meetings with the customer generated lists of actions and responsible parties to execute them. The teams put in place matrices to measure the number of bugs encountered, time for bug resolution, and outstanding unfixed bugs, and then the board reviewed them. As ever, you get what you measure. Before long, the attention of so many influential executives generated significant quality improvement.

- **Supply-chain issues**—A specific manager was allocated to the customer's account. All of his orders were given attention to ensure the matrices the companies jointly developed achieved improvement and maintained a level of performance acceptable to the customer. When delays did occur, particularly with important orders, ad hoc task forces formed to rectify the situation.

- **Joint Marketing**—The companies established a joint marketing fund to enable the companies to comarket. A number of their products were cobranded. They were taken to market not only by joint high-touch sales teams but also through the telco's mass-market infrastructure for small/medium enterprise and indirectly through the sales company's other channel partners. Imagine the upside for both companies in terms of their ability to address new customers and markets. In addition to the more obvious below-the-line marketing efforts, the teams were able to address above-the-line opportunities by constructing specialized teams to target midmarket customers through market research and subsequent targeted calling. The board tasked marketing directors from both sides with building a marketing plan and executing against it. They expended effort to properly measure the success of the various initiatives to ensure they achieved their requisite bang for the buck.

- **Sales from the telco to the sales company**—Both companies were naturally keen to stay on the right side of reciprocal trading regulations. That said, it was reasonable for the sales company to give the telco access to information about upcoming requirements and relevant expectations associated with it. This allowed the telco to have an extremely well-managed account with top high-level executive access (exactly what this book addresses). As a result, it was able to compete effectively in terms of procurement. As you'd expect, the telco took normal part in requests for proposals, so it had at least a fair chance, even when it didn't win.

Governance

As you can see, it was most important for the telco to drive its sales into the market, and this imperative shaped the governance structure. It demonstrated how putting the customer's needs at the forefront enables good decision making and creates the right mechanisms for mutual success.

In this case, the senior vice presidents responsible for country sales from both companies jointly chaired the executive board. They sat over a team that primarily consisted of sales leaders from the various market segments, as well as representatives from engineering, supply chain, and marketing.

At every meeting, the emphasis was on setting sales targets and measuring progress against them. Team members reviewed large deals and settled disputes. Inevitably, channel conflicts caused by third-party vendors (from the telco's perspective) and secondary channels (from the sales company's perspective) occurred. So the team invented and systemized what it called a traffic-lighting system. Using this system, it could address opportunities without causing conflict among the various sales teams. In essence, every opportunity on the companies' common database would go through the traffic-lighting system as indicated in the following chart.

Table 4.8
Traffic-Lighting System for Addressing Sales Opportunities in Strategic Accounts

Opportunity State	Description
Red	The opportunity is addressed with a third party—either another vendor or another channel. No further action is required. The possibility of a dispute is eliminated because of an upfront decision not to engage. (This is instead of the normal approach involving a lack of clarity and subsequent fighting between teams unsure of their opposite's intent.)
Amber	This account requires more discovery work, and, as a result, the teams keep their options open. Depending on the circumstances surrounding the opportunity, they set a time limit to make a red/green decision.
Green	The joint teams address this opportunity exclusively without involving other parties. Green opportunities are key areas of focus.

In principle, green-light opportunities should be increasing in number, while red and amber should be diminishing.

Not only was this traffic lighting a key tool in preventing disputes, but the teams also used it to indicate how well (or badly) teams were working together. Each quarterly board meeting was well publicized, with content and presentations sent out a week in advance. All the heads of the working groups were invited, and while the meetings emphasized sales progress, the members representing every other facet of the relationship—quality, supply chain, marketing, and so on—presented their areas and reported their progress against their respective matrices.

In addition, both sides obtained executive sponsorship. In the case of the sales company, the sponsoring leader was the executive vice president for the entire region, and for the telco, it was the vice president responsible for the company's national operation. Both attended bi-quarterly meetings and took a keen interest in its progress, bringing in high-level support. (You'll remember the executive VP for R&D took executive sponsorship of the quality initiative.) As a result, a surprising number of high-profile leaders from both companies took an interest in the relationship between the companies.

Regular high-level focus of this nature brings results, and this case was no exception. Improvements at all levels were experienced, and both companies ended up referencing the relationship as a global best practice to be replicated with other vendors and suppliers. Sales to and through the customer telco multiplied dramatically, and quality, supply-chain, and even pricing issues improved.

There's little doubt that, as the relationship deepened and the customer's perception of value increased, the sensitivity to price started to decrease. This is a clear example of selling value while getting away from commoditization.

Conclusions

Can you see the importance of concentration of resources into key accounts where there's a significant return for your efforts?

The idea is to use high-touch account management to build deep relationships that add value to your customer. This operates not only at the functional level but also by becoming part of the customer's business, thus delivering both efficiencies and competitive advantage. Every company has limited resources, so swarming all of your accounts is not practical. Be selective, and pick your targets carefully.

Given excellent targeting and execution on your strategic accounts, you'll move away from being a vendor of commodities and toward becoming a trusted advisor and strategic partner. Your revenues and margins will improve as your customers recognize the value of your strategic relationship.

5 High-Competitive Readiness

Our army's combat readiness, its morale, cohesion of military groups, the results of combat training and efficient development of new technology, which our troops are receiving more and more of, are directly dependent on you.—**Vladimir Putin**, *president of Russia, on June 28, 2012, talking at the Kremlin to honors graduates from the General Staff Academy*

You can't overestimate the need to plan and prepare. In most of the mistakes I've made, there has been this common theme of inadequate planning beforehand. You really can't over-prepare in business!—**Chris Corrigan,** managing director of the Patrick Corporation

The Russian armed forces have a principle of war called high combat readiness, which is a measure of how quickly their troops can react to any given threat or opportunity. It's about training, manning, organization, logistics (ammunition, spare parts, fuel and lubricants, etc.), and transportation, both strategic and tactical, to get a concentration of forces to the *schwerpunkt* quickly and in a state that they can achieve rapid victory.

Such high preparedness was a lesson the Russians learned from bitter experience. In World War II, they were caught unawares and unready by the German invasion in Operation Barbarossa. While such preparations seem like common sense and to be taken for granted, massive effort and cost are associated with having large numbers of troops at high combat readiness. The military must expend huge resources to maintain fleets of vehicles and weapons; large stockpiles of fuel and ammunition are expensive to buy and store; and training, motivating, and maintaining standing armies presents a colossal challenge. What appears to be an obvious precaution comes at an enormous price.

Applying this principle of readiness to the sales environment is highly instructive. In business, we're constantly in the fray, competing for deals in a dynamic battlefield. Thus, it's much easier for us to be motivated to ensure we're in a continual state of readiness to react to opportunities and threats as they arise. However, I'm continually surprised at how poorly sales teams are prepared to take on the challenges of competition in the marketplace. I'm not sure whether this occurs due to complacency or bad leadership, or both.

This chapter addresses the critical areas of sending your sales teams into battle and maintaining their preparedness. Remember, it's not a one-off exercise; competitive readiness is an ongoing process that needs to be top of mind for all sales leaders and their teams.

Training

Everyone I know thinks training of sales teams is important, and of course *I* do because it's how I make my living. So I find it astonishing that, in most businesses, sales teams are trained in unstructured, confused, and inconsistent ways.

Poorly trained sales teams are often manifestations of badly thought-out go-to-market strategies. Companies that give unclear messages to the market typically also have sales teams that don't clearly understand their value proposition. So by correcting the structure of your sales training, you'll force improvements in the overall quality of your messaging to the market.

Structuring Sales Training

First, review your overall sales plan. Refresh your memory on exactly what you want your teams to achieve and, consequently, how you need to train them. Before training can begin, however, it's important to structure all of the data and messaging that's available to the troops.

Generically speaking, the quadrant diagram that follows synthesizes the balance between data and complexity of messaging necessary in preparing for sales training.

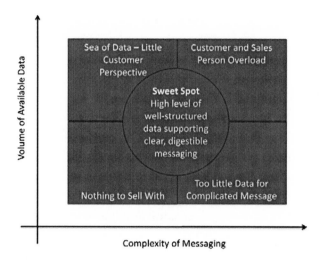

Figure 5.1. Balance of Data and Complexity

On the vertical axis, I plot the amount of data available to the sales-person. *Availability* is a key here; data is not considered available if it's in binders locked in a library. Nowadays, we'd expect it to be available on the company Intranet, but that's not enough either. Data needs to be searchable and structured in a way that people can find it. Salespeople aren't renowned for their patience, so if information is hard to locate, slow to download, or hard to understand, it's not considered available data.

In the field of high technology, not only is the amount of data huge, but it's constantly changing and growing. This presents a challenge because, even with the best will in the world, salespeople simply won't keep up with masses of complex (and boring) data sheets posted on the Intranet in a relatively unstructured way. Rather, it needs to be structured into a form of hierarchy. That means the sales teams can go to top-level generic information and drill down to more detail as required.

Perhaps there's a rumbling of unrest among sales traditionalists at this point. I can hear them saying, "We don't need a bunch of information on 'speeds and feeds.' That's the job of the sales engineers and techni-cians. We need to talk to the customer about benefits and value proposi-tions." And, certainly, we don't want sales teams trained to such a level of technical competence that they think they can rush into a customer's data center with soldering iron in hand. But I'm 100 percent convinced that strong product and technical knowledge are critical for any salesperson. (This is discussed in more detail under product training, but in the meantime, keep in mind that a certain level of technical competence is a major part of the art of selling.)

On the horizontal axis is plotted the complexity of the messaging required to be passed to the customer. This is important from a training perspective because if the value proposition is too complex for the sales teams to understand, then they certainly won't be able to articulate it to the customer. Before any training can begin, be sure to have hierarchical, accessible data and messaging that's digestible for the average salesperson.

At the top right corner of the diagram, you'll see masses of product and service data and a highly complex set of messages to the customer. At this point, your sales team will melt down and be completely unable to articulate anything sensible to the customer. They'll become too reliant on technical staff and be reduced to arranging meetings and trying to understand the customer's org chart—the lifebelt for account managers who simply don't know how to add value. This is no way to become a trusted advisor—or even someone who can comment sensibly on how the company's products and services can provide benefit to the customer.

I've encountered this situation with companies that supply highly complex software solutions for billing and product analysis for service providers. The products themselves are extensive, generating a lot of data-sheet material, and the messaging for the customer is equally voluminous. The salespeople find it nearly impossible to synthesize a story that can be told quickly (the elevator brief you'll learn about). Plus they're certainly not capable of talking in detail about the product and how it can bring competitive advantage to their customer. As far as that customer is concerned, an air of mystery tends to hang over the company and its products. Value gets overlooked simply due to a lack of understanding.

The bottom right in the diagram represents a company with a lot of complex information about how they can benefit their customers but with little product information. In this situation, the customer will be asking, "Where's the beef?" The "beef" refers to documentation, data sheets, case studies, and more. Typically, the company will rely on demonstrations of the product to provide information on its utility. In most cases, though, the sales team can't provide the demonstrations and need to rely on technicians. If this situation is allowed to continue, the sales team can become alienated from the customer.

This is a classic situation with start-up software companies that are long on product but short on documentation. The products are frequently labyrinthine and therefore difficult to explain. Often, little thought has gone into the actual messaging to the client. Benefit statements are long and rambling. Because little collateral exists in terms of solid product information, the whole thing feels flaky to the customer. The salespeople have no way of redressing the balance.

The bottom left corner of the diagram represents a hopeless situation. The salesperson has no product data to speak of, and the sales department hasn't produced any messaging. Salespeople have nothing to work on, and so nothing can happen from a sales perspective. The situation sounds unlikely, but it's typical of a lot of start-ups, particularly in the hardware business. In hardware, a bunch of technologists come up with an excellent box of electronics, but no one has even the faintest idea of how to take it to market. There's no point in even employing, let alone training, salespeople until this situation is rectified.

At top left is a scenario in which a lot of effort has gone into producing product data, but a hole exists in how the product is messaged to the client. Benefit statements and value propositions are absent, and the salespeople are essentially asked to talk about "speeds and feeds" rather than positioning competitive advantage to their clients. This inevitably drives them down the chain of command of their customers' organizations, forcing them to have conversations with the technical folks rather than key decision makers.

This situation tends to arise in well-established hardware firms. There, the teams have had time to document their products from a data-sheet perspective, but they don't have the expertise to address the customer-messaging piece.

Here's the sweet spot in terms of preparation for training—the middle position of this scenario. As a sales leader, be sure that relevant, well-structured collateral is available on both axes to ensure you can effectively train your teams.

Product Data

As companies grow, their product data tend to become more voluminous and inaccessible to salespeople. In turn, salespeople quickly become confused and bored while trying to fight through the complexity. Yet vast quantities of products and options with requisite data sheets are a necessary part of our high-technology market. But without structure, they can't be used effectively as sales tools.

The answer lies in organization of data, and of course Web technology helps a great deal here. The Web makes it easy to divide products into generic groups and associate various layers of drill down into more and more detail. Adding multimedia content, specifically video, to demystify and enliven the material also helps. This way, both customers and sales teams are provided with a vibrant and easy-to-navigate set of documents—a far cry from the binder full of data sheets they used to take on sales calls.

So many examples of how this can be achieved are on the Web that I encourage you to look for yourself. Find examples in your own industry and segments and study them.

That said, let's use Cisco as an example of best practice. This company was a first mover and innovator in terms of using the Web for internal and external users, and it remains at the top. A visit to cisco.com provides you with a view on how a market leader organizes an incredible amount of product data into highly digestible structures featuring attractive multimedia content.

Site-specific search engines are still an area of weakness. Salespeople and customers need to be able to type short descriptions of what they're looking for and get a succinct list of relevant links that will help them. (I have yet to see this well executed on the microscale of a company Intranet or Internet site.)

I've mixed the discussion of customer and internal data because your sales teams and customers largely have access to the same product data. If you get it right for your customers, it will be right for the sales teams. You could have no better incentive for investment in this area.

Customer Messaging

At this point, let's address the challenge of how you wrap up all of the low-level product detail and find a way to present it to a customer at multiple levels of an organization. It stands to reason that the people who make up the shop-floor end of an organization—the techies in a data center, for example—need a more product-centric set of messages than those in the CxO suite. At that top level, a more benefits-oriented pitch is appropriate. I refer to the product-centric, lower-level messaging as micro level and the high-end CxO suite briefings as macro level.

For the micro level, be sure to summarize the nature and key benefits of products and services quickly. It's tough to give generic direction about how products should be grouped for this purpose, but take the example of BT Global Services' excellent YouTube channel, BT Viewpoint.* There, the company posts sixty-second videos delivered by professional presenters on a vast range of individual and product groups.

For example, you can see an overview on cybersecurity, along with a collection of more focused summaries of its component parts (e.g., managed firewalls, ethical hacking, denial of service mitigation, etc.). Of course, included are detailed data sheets, white papers, case studies, and micro sites for each product (the product data), but these messaging videos nicely sum up what a salesperson should be pitching at various levels of the customer company. BT makes these videos available to both its staff and customers, and they've proven to be invaluable training and sales aids.

At the same time, learn to tell a macro-level story about your company, products, and services that you can deliver quickly. Your message should provide two or three clear ideas and be highly memorable. While excellent salespeople will be able to naturally put this story together in their heads, you'll need to teach the majority of your team members a smooth version of this. In fact, getting this macro story right is a critical prerequisite to training.

The main components of a good macro-level story include answers to the following questions:

---

*   http://www.youtube.com/feed/UCUl23HHqQ48T-kwAf9V6GfA

- Who are we?

- What do we do?

- Why is it relevant to you?

- What benefits do we deliver to you?

- Why are we better than others?

Let's stay with BT Global Services as an example. In this context, this is a macro-level pitch at the CEO level with an aim of providing security solutions:

We are one of the largest service providers in the world providing network, IT solutions, and professional services in 197 countries. We have a wide range of managed security services that would address your current concerns without having to invest in manpower or equipment. We are recognized as a Gartner magic quadrant leader and could tailor a solution for you across your global footprint.

There's no doubt about it; the message is short, sharp, easy to deliver, and highly memorable—for the salesperson and the customer.

At CIO level, the level of abstraction goes down a notch:

We have a wide range of managed security solutions provided across our global network, which provide a range of cloud-based platforms such as DDOS mitigation and threat monitoring as well as premise-based services such as managed firewalls, host/network intrusion prevention, and network access. We are recognized for our innovation and quality by Gartner and have an installed base of thousands of international customers. Our approach would mean low to zero investment in manpower and equipment, rapid deployment, and an OPEX approach to the provision of a suite of security services. The risk of failure to implement the service and maintain it successfully would be massively mitigated by the fact that the solutions are ready made, deployable now, and accompanied by service-level agreements. (Note: OPEX is operational expenditure.)

The same messages are contained here, but in the second, more detail is added because the CIO will be more familiar with the requirements, technology, and terminology.

From here on in, the messaging gets more fragmented, but the hierarchy remains the same. It's a good idea to look at BT Viewpoint to get a feel for how the company deals with it. The site offers overviews of the security portfolio and then individual groupings of products. It presents a top-level account of the products and services, but it focuses on why the customer should be talking to BT and the benefits the product provides. Here is a paraphrased example:

BT's managed security appliances reside in your network but are controlled 24/7, 365 days a year from BT's global operation centers. Problems are proactively solved before you, as a customer, even know about them, and attacks are repelled before any damage can be done or data lost. Performance is guaranteed by a service-level agreement, and customer care is provided by a single point of contact who will not only manage your problems but assist you with innovation, upgrade, and sun-setting of end-of-life equipment or underutilized services. The key benefits are enhanced protection, savings on IT staff, and the elimination of CAPEX on equipment. The whole offer is provided as a service and can be charged to OPEX. (Note: CAPEX is capital expenditure and OPEX is operational expenditure.)

Let me add a small government health warning so as not to create confusion: not every customer is eager to lower CAPEX and increase OPEX, but this trend is evident, and it does mean that technology can be refreshed regularly without having to constantly demand new CAPEX budgets.

Execution of Training

After having put together the materials to get you into that sweet spot of structured training, you next must figure out how to effectively deliver the training. You may find this challenging, and the execution will vary from situation to situation.

First, accept that salespeople will avoid reading documents, viewing videos, attending courses and presentations, or doing anything else that distracts them from whatever they believe they should be doing. Never accept the age-old excuse "I've got a customer meeting" whenever training or testing comes up. Make sure you give people plenty of notice, and then use your authority to force them to attend.

Maslow's hierarchy of needs indicates that all of us (yes, even salespeople) seek self-improvement as a key life goal. The trick to getting teams to pay attention to training and be motivated to absorb and apply the material is to show them how it will help them do their jobs better.

Salespeople in the field of high technology have become far too reliant on sales engineers to talk about technology. I knew a contact-center technology expert who used to tell account managers, "Let me do all the talking; you just pay for lunch." The problem is that if you technologically emasculate your salespeople, the relationship with the account becomes highly technical due to the dominance of sales engineers in all conversations. Therefore, it becomes subject to commoditization, preventing you from approaching the high-touch level being espoused.

I acknowledge that the salespeople will never know more than the engineers, but they do need to get a grip on the product sets and associated messaging. The whole point of the sweet spot is that once you've put together effective sales materials, your role is to make sure they're used as intended.

True, you can lead a horse to water, but you can't make him drink. However, it's crucial to ensure that sales teams take training seriously and internalize as much information as possible. After all, they put themselves in a position to present, discuss, and position the material at all levels of their customers' businesses.

Typically, training will involve the assimilation of data and messaging, hopefully in sweet-spot format. It will include instructor-led sessions, webcasts, and self study of multimedia materials. To get salespeople to do things they don't want to do, appeal to their inner demons—greed and competitiveness.

To verify that the salespeople have learned and understood the material, test them using some combination of the following methods:

Examination—Create multiple-choice tests, and continually update them with changes in products and messages. Require the salespeople to take and pass these tests. Note: I strongly suggest that, even if the test is online, you make sure to proctor the environment. Otherwise, salespeople will cheat by getting sales engineers to take the test for them. This doesn't make them bad; it's just that salespeople are the ultimate pragmatists and survivors. They'll do whatever it takes to succeed as long as they can get away with it.

It makes sense to tie exam success to payments of incentives. Either you can hold back commission payments until exams are passed or you can pay direct incentives for passing the exam. Be clear about your contractual position. As soon as you talk about wallet-affecting matters, greed kicks in. You'll quickly get the attention you need from the sales teams. Publishing of league tables to indicate scores also encourages healthy competition and incites fear of humiliation among the teams. Do, however, be careful about your companies' human resources policies before applying this technique.

Presentation—Having salespeople give presentations to peers and supervisors works well to ensure they've learned the information. Typically, I tell individuals to prepare to present three topics each, usually with an appropriate customer scenario associated with each subject. I bring the team together and then get each person to present one of the topics in front of the group. I'm always surprised at how many salespeople dislike public speaking and find this type of activity incredibly stressful. However, they need to face the fact that if they can't perform in this relatively safe environment, they'll never make it in front of the customer. These sessions can be uncomfortably revealing.

I also find the need to compete with colleagues and look good in front of the leadership team ensures learning. Typically, attractive prizes of tablets, smartphones, or media players make the whole effort more exciting and take away some of the pain team members may feel.

Customer simulation—This is done most effectively with third parties acting as customers in carefully prepared scenarios. They can be highly instructive for the teams, especially when used to address specific issues companies are experiencing in the market. For example, I saw great messaging worked out using these simulations when a US company was taking a severe beating from its customers as a result of low pricing from a Chinese competitor. The salespeople were taught the necessary rebuttals and counterarguments and given a chance to hone them in a relatively safe environment before coming under fire in the market. This remarkably successful approach filled the sales teams with confidence and gave the market a clear set of consistent messages about the realities of the pricing situation.

It's extremely useful to video record these simulations. While many people feel uncomfortable watching themselves perform, the ability to see yourself as others see you is extremely powerful. It can lead to significant improvements in customer-handling techniques and message delivery.

Motivation

A key factor in high-competitive readiness is to ensure the sales teams are strongly motivated for success. The discussion about offensive spirit, for example, shows how this serves to energize people and drive aggressive behavior. Nurturing this atmosphere inside the team is utterly invaluable in motivating the salespeople. In addition, they need to be prepared to leave a bit of themselves in the marketplace while winning the battle to close business.

Let's look at a few techniques that help ensure team members are ready to throw themselves into the fight.

Pay Plan

In Maslow's hierarchy of needs, compensation is near the base of the triangle and considered a survival need. Salespeople are decidedly interested in how much money they can put in their pockets. However, to some extent, this interest is caused by the fact that, in sales, commission is a good way of keeping score, and high earnings are associated with good performance, recognition, and respect of others. That puts these needs closer to the top of the hierarchy approaching self-actualization.

In any case, for a number of reasons, getting the right compensation is a key motivator.

Consider the following outputs for your compensation scheme:

- **Sales-order value**—the value of the purchase orders received

- **Revenue**—the value of invoiced deals

- **Margin**—most typically, the net margin earned

- **Discount**—This one is a bit tricky, tied as it is to margin. Most companies endeavor to compensate individuals for keeping their overall discounting within certain bands.

- **Collections**—Many companies rely on their salespeople to collect cash from their customers. In these cases, an element of compensation is tied to cash received and the timely manner in which it's collected.

Although no set formula exists for the perfect scheme, you'll find the following series of guidelines useful.

On-Target Earnings (OTE)—This key number is the earnings target you expect a successful salesperson to reach at the end of the period. Two components are involved:

- **Basic salary**—This refers to what the salesperson is paid, whether he or she sells anything or not. This can be anything from 0 to 80 percent of OTE, depending on the circumstances. An approximate norm in the high-tech industry is 50 percent, which attracts high-caliber talent but keeps the sales teams hungry for success.

- **Commission**—At its crudest, commission is paid as a percentage of sales made, but this is oversimplistic in most environments. It's more common to set a target and pay salespeople on achievement of this goal, typically on a quarterly basis.

Be cautious with the following:

- **Target setting**—You need to know the customer base well so you can stretch the teams to achieve the business you believe the market offers. However, if the target is too high, it will be seen as unachievable. The salespeople will give up, leave, or shelter sales in the period until the following period (when they'll be more valuable proportionally in reaching a lower target). All of that is bad news that can be avoided by sensible target allocations.

- **Overachievement**—You don't want salespeople to reach their targets and then stop selling. Momentum can be easily lost and difficult to regain. With this in mind, compensating people for overachievement make sense. Commonly, this is done with accelerators, or pay at an enhanced level of commission for sales made above target. Although accelerators depend on circumstances, a typical scale looks like this:

Table 5.1

Typical Accelerators for Overachievement Beyond Target

Level of Achievement Against Target	Accelerated Rate of Commission
101–110%	125%
111–120%	150%
>120%	175%

The examples in the chart are aggressive. It's crucial to set targets carefully. If they're too low, you'll end up with a payment bonanza for average performance; if they're too high, you'll kill the desire to achieve accelerators because it's too difficult. That said, paying out at this level can be highly motivating for salespeople. When used correctly, it can help generate excellent results.

- **Control**—Setting a sales-order value target without careful controls in place is dangerous. You'll quickly find your levels of discounts running out of control. Consider these options:

  o Place tight controls on salespeople, giving them narrow bands of discount with which to negotiate, allowing deviation from these levels only with special permission and sign-off.

  o Band commission rates to allow salespeople to fight for higher pricing to earn higher commission. What is the logical conclusion to this? Out-of-band discounting on the downside will lead to zero commission. But do legislate against this happening rather than assume salespeople will figure it out themselves.

- **Unexpected consequences**—Look out for the difficulties associated with not including your expected outputs of revenue and collections. So far, only sales-order value and discount levels (and margin, as a consequence) have been discussed. Consider these problems:

  o Revenue can be an issue insofar as overeager salespeople will close deals with customers long before the customer needs equipment—most commonly because a building or data center is not ready. A deal is made between the customer and salesperson to achieve better pricing, free equipment, licenses, and so on. To prevent this, most schemes don't pay out until orders actually generate revenue (i.e., the equipment ships and the invoices are cut). To further discourage this type of behavior, orders on the books for a certain length of time (three months, for example) are simply cancelled.

  o Take collections into account to discourage sales to insolvent or slow-paying customers. Most companies run careful and ongoing credit checks on customers to prevent this from happening anyway. However, as an extra layer of security and to ensure salesperson involvement in the collection process, it makes sense to hold a commission payment until collections are completed. Be careful not to make this overly punitive. In some environments, customers routinely withhold 10 percent of invoice amounts for twelve months to act as a reserve in case of poor performance or delivery issues. It seems unreasonable to not pay salespeople on these amounts. In general, however, tying sales compensation to customer payments is wise.

When implementing a scheme, you're dealing with a complicated set of issues, and most companies evolve complicated sets of documentation around their individual pay plans. They do this to protect the company and its shareholders from deviant behavior from the sales teams. However, in reality, this defeats the point of the commission plan—to motivate the salespeople. Salespeople probably won't be motivated by something they don't understand, let alone something they can't be bothered to read.

What is the bottom line? Keep your plan as simple as possible, and continually explain it to your sales team. It's a major leadership challenge but one that can make a huge difference.

Recognition

Without wishing to overplay Maslow's hierarchy of needs, esteem is at the penultimate layer before the pinnacle of the pyramid. Self-esteem, confidence, and respect of others are well above compensation in terms of their importance to individuals. This point is lost in many companies where the selling process turns into a passionless meat grinder focused on targets and commissions.

In most cases, the selling process is about the formation of relationships, the creation of win-win stories, the celebration of value propositions, the matching of customer needs to company capabilities and technology, the resultant savings in customer costs, and the enhancement of competitive advantage. When sales are abundant, the process is a beautiful thing. On the other hand, the selling effort can be painful and fruitless. (As I tell sales teams, you have to kiss a lot of frogs before you find a prince.) Therefore, it's well worth celebrating and publicizing your successes.

Consider these benefits:

- Successful individuals receive the adulation and respect of their colleagues. (I suspect most people in the audience are secretly seething with jealousy, but they're motivated to be on stage next time.) This recognition provides a massive boost to an individual's morale and motivation. When a note goes around or an announcement is made about a team's success, if anyone is left off the list of participants (regrettably, often one of the sales engineers), a flurry of complaints occurs until the overlooked person gets a special mention. It sounds childish, but I can assure you that in every geographical theater I've worked, adults zealously seek mention and public acclaim for their actions. It's incredibly motivating.

- Sharing success motivates people to do well and gain similar publicity for their own efforts.

- Where teams have applied successful formulae, it's highly beneficial to share their approaches with others. Many companies I've worked with have embraced this approach in their culture. As a result, they build a database of best practices, which they publish on their Intranet. This encourages teams to cross-reference their strategies for account success.

The methods of recognition are quite varied and tend to be hierarchical. The following ideas work well and provide an escalating path of reward and esteem:

- Send out regular "Win of the Week" e-mails to the team. It's simple and effective. Speak to the account manager to ensure all participants are mentioned and an effective description of the win is included. I like to see discussion around differentiation strategy, how the competition was defeated, and what benefits the customer gleaned.

- Present prizes at sales meetings. You can award teams with anything from glassware to tablet computers and smartphones. (The prize isn't that important; the photograph of the team shaking hands with the boss and the round of applause count most.) It's good to accompany the ceremony with a short presentation on the win by the account manager. Again, encourage the manager to emphasize the critical win themes and mention everyone on the team.

- Hold an annual competition in which you recognize outstanding individuals from sales and engineering in some form of platinum club. That club might involve going with partners to an exotic location to spend time with senior executives of the company. Cynics may say this sounds more like a punishment than a reward, but it has nothing to do with sipping martinis on the veranda of a five-star hotel in Waikiki with the chairman. Rather, it's about knowing that everyone back home realizes you have done well and deserve to be recognized and respected.

Whichever way you look at it, recognition has a huge positive effect on motivation and is critical to creating competitive readiness in the sales force.

Team Building

The idea of a team is critical to competitive readiness, so build an atmosphere in which people cooperate with one another in a seamless way. Because salespeople are by nature selfish and highly competitive, you're faced with creating a tricky balance—that is, an environment in which individuals compete to be the best but still want to cooperate with one another to succeed. (The next chapter on leadership and maintenance of morale discusses this at some length.)

Use three key methods to build this environment:

- **General approach of the sales leader**—Constantly talk about the importance of teamwork, and stress the need for the troops to cooperate with one another. Whenever you have a chance to walk the walk and demonstrate how teamwork leads to success, do so—then tell everybody about it. Never take credit for success; always emphasize the key role the team has played in any win or forward movement.

- **Team meetings**—Pulling the team together regularly is critical. You're almost certainly going to run forecast calls every week, but bringing the entire team together (engineers, salespeople, administrators, etc.) at least once a month also makes sense. You can vary the agenda month to month, but be sure to take each of these actions:
  o Review how the team is doing against its numeric and soft objectives.
  o Catch up on new products, strategies, and plan changes.
  o Recognize strong performances and feature presentations on how people achieved them.
  o Provide opportunities to ask questions and to give and discuss answers.

The atmosphere needs to be light rather than oppressive. Deliver tough messages in a way that encourages improvement rather than admonishes the guilty. When handled well, these meetings result in bonding for the team as members form a sense of common purpose. On the other hand, if the team doesn't come together regularly, selfish, isolated behavior that can ultimately destroy team spirit can flourish.

Today, many teams are spread over such wide geographies that bringing them together in one place is not practical. So find ways of using video to bridge these distance gaps. You have multiple choices, starting with Skype and working up to high-bandwidth Telepresence. Whatever you choose, it will be a lot more scalable and cost-effective than flying people to meetings.

Web-conferencing solutions such as Live Meeting and Webex also provide the capabilities to show presentation slides, instant message among participants, ask questions by text, and poll multiple users, creating a much more interactive experience. The more expensive the solution, the more immersive—and therefore effective—the meetings will be. That said, teams learn to work well with whatever technology is available to them. Expect people to adapt to audio or video conferences and get plenty of benefit from the meeting.

- **Team-building events**—In most cases, photographs people put on their desks or cubicle walls are images of team-building events. Sometimes I feel cynical about the return on investment of spending time and money off-site taking part in leisure activities, but I have to admit these occasions do draw teams together. The quality of events varies, but given a good subcontractor to run the team building for you, it's surprising how much benefit you can gain. Certainly don't dismiss the idea until you've researched your options.

Conclusion

If you can execute well on pay plans and commissions, recognition, and team building, you're well on the way to having a superbly motivated team. Combine these with first-class materials and good training, and you'll have a high level of competitive readiness that will stand you in excellent stead.

Leadership and the Maintenance of Morale

The morale of the soldier is the most important single factor in war.—**Field Marshall Bernard Montgomery**, *Commander, British Eighth Army, 1942*

Morale is good; troops are confident; leaders are capable.—**General John Abizaid,** *commander of the United States Central Command, 2003*

Morale is a key factor in success, both on the battlefield and in the marketplace. A team with high morale will be energized with offensive spirit and able to achieve great things. To me, it's about energy, enthusiasm, courage, can-do attitude, perseverance, team spirit, and hard work. That's quite a list, but it's more than possible to achieve in a team that's riding a wave of high morale.

Where does high morale come from? How can we as business managers create it? For me, the answer is, quite simply, effective leadership. While that's a simple answer, however, it's difficult to achieve.

My favorite personality in business leadership is Ford's CEO, Alan Mulally, who has been at the helm of the motor giant during its turnaround into profit. He came to Ford from the Boeing Company as an industry outsider and, as you can imagine, was greeted by a fair degree of cynicism. He discovered a culture of silos and fiefdoms and a lack of transparency at all levels, leading to rock-bottom morale and consequent dysfunction.

Just as we saw with General Montgomery, Mulally, buzzing with energy, set about breaking down barriers. He completely opened up business information for everyone to see in the areas of research and

As an example of leadership affecting morale, consider General Montgomery during 1942 in North Africa. When he was appointed as the new commander of the British Eighth Army, the morale of the soldiers was very low. They had taken quite a battering at the hands of the German Afrika Korps under Rommel, and the overall atmosphere in the ranks was one of lethargy, melancholy, and defeatism.

To get a grip on the situation, Montgomery set about his task in a flurry of energy and frenetic activity. He fired ineffective officers, made sure that the entire army plan was personally briefed by him down to low-level commanders, and got out to his units all over the desert to motivate and inspire the troops.

As he said in his report on the campaign, "I was determined that the soldiers should go into this battle in a high state of enthusiasm."

While Montgomery's overall generalship capability is sometimes questioned by historians, I am full of admiration for his ability to transfer energy and a will to win to his subordinates at all levels and, as a result, drive and maintain high morale. It's a great example of how raw leadership can invigorate an entire army—and a crossover exists in business.

development, manufacturing, and sales. He included cross-functional elements in meetings and refused to use business data as a weapon, instead using the data as a tool to instigate improvement. All this enhanced team spirit and raised morale.

"It would be far less effective for this process to be just about me," he said. "I wasn't going to succeed if my team didn't succeed." He also made sure he built a culture of transparency and embraced performance indicators. He broke down the opaque approach that had previously existed and emphasized teams, not individuals. Finally, he made sure the plan was communicated to all.

With these actions, Mulally led Ford out of the 2007 crisis of the Detroit automakers with flying colors, well ahead of his crosstown rivals.

A key building block in military officer training came from John Adair, a lecturer in the 1970s at Sandhurst, the British Army's Royal Military Academy. In his book *Effective Leadership,* Adair established a leadership model of three interlocking circles, which provide key areas of focus that any officer or manager needs to address simultaneously:

- Task need

- Group need

- Individual need

Let me analyze each of these areas to emphasize the role and nature of leadership over and above those of management. Without going into too much detail, I'll tell you about an old commanding officer of mine when I was serving in Germany. He was one of the last serving officers who'd been in World War II and had led a platoon during the D-Day landings in 1944. For him, managers were people who developed a plan involving pain and sacrifice without any consultation. He then promulgated the plan by sticking it up on the notice board (an Intranet page nowadays). A leader, on the other hand, would develop the plan in a collaborative way (not necessarily achieving consensus, of course) and then brief the teams face-to-face to achieve buy in, understanding, and motivation. My former CO adequately described the importance of leadership in terms of driving high morale. You can also see the collaborative qualities of Montgomery and Mulally in these descriptions and figure out why I chose those two individuals as inspiring leadership role models.

Task Need—We've reviewed planning and objective setting earlier. In the context of leadership, this definition of the overall task in front of the team is key. In his book, Adair explained that definition, planning, and briefing are important elements of leadership and critical to the success of any task. That means to make sure you're consulting widely as you define the task and build the plan. Afterward, make sure to brief the team well. Where face-to-face is impossible, leverage communication modes—print, audio, Web, and video conferencing—to get your message across and ensure that everyone understands how it applies to the task ahead.

Group Need—Teamwork is vital in sales, and as a leader, nurturing the growth of the group in the context of achieving the task is important. Adair discussed controlling, evaluating, motivating, and organizing as key leadership functions vis-à-vis the group. Earlier, we addressed the importance of timely business information in terms of continually monitoring the performance of the team. We also mentioned the need to make course changes and organizational upgrades as well as to weed out poor performers and recognize excellence to get a group together to achieve a common goal. In addition, who you are and what you do are important. The group will expect you to set an example in the way you behave in the office and in front of customers, how you dress, what time you come and go from work, your self-sacrifice and dedication to the group, and more. Like it or not, you're a role model, and the group will watch your every move. More than that, group members will subconsciously absorb these factors, thus affecting their own behavior.

Individual Need—Once again, controlling, evaluating, and motivating are important to fulfill an individual's needs related to the overall environment. All the people on your team have the right to know what's expected of them and how they're performing against those expectations. In sales, we have the fabulously clear indicator of numbers performance against target. A good leader will use this with other SMART objectives to provide feedback required to enhance individual performance. It's a lot more than that, though; individuals, particularly the younger team members, need mentorship across the board to fulfill their individual needs.

You likely remember starting in sales and having a veteran first-line sales manager who helped you with everything from how to dress and how to pack your cars with samples and collateral to handling objections, product knowledge, etc. These leaders were always pressing to come on sales calls as a way to assist and monitor performance while providing pre- and post-call briefings and analysis. Such mentoring is vital to individual growth and development; it feeds into group and task performance.

Conclusion

I hope you find the idea of leadership, its application in military and sales environments, the maintenance of high morale, and the examples of how it works highly inspirational. We've read about the amazing sacrifices men and women make in wartime, the courage they show, and the actions they take. For me, it's exciting how good leadership, teamwork, and individual effort come together to achieve equally astonishing results in the peacetime sales environment. Is that true for you, too?

7 Unity of Command

Nothing in war is more important than unity of command. Thus when war is waged against a single power there must be but one army, acting on one line and led by one chief. ... Better one bad general than two good ones.—**Napoleon Bonaparte**, *1805, seven years before invading Russia*

Each worker should have only one boss with no other conflicting lines of command.—**Henri Fayol**, *1916, one of the influential early contributors to modern management theory*

In the military, unity of command is sacrosanct; all forces act under one responsible commander, which is an effective way of massing resources to achieve maximum combat power. The rigors of battle demand that one commander has the authority to direct all available forces to achieve a common objective.

I'm a strong believer in applying this principle of unity of command to business. The best results are achieved when companies put all of their resources under a single commander who strives for a set of common objectives with all available resources under that commander's control.

These days in sales, we see more and more matrix organizations due to the complexity of technology as well as vertical and geographic fragmentation. To show this, let's look at an example of the use of matrix organization and the disasters it creates for the sales effort. We'll examine an IT company in a particular geography (a country in the Arabian Gulf) and the mess created by failing to provide unity of command.

First, although the geography leader had control of the actual sales-people, the sales engineers were managed from a different country altogether. This immediately caused problems because, as you know, dif-

An excellent example of unity of command was in the Soviet advance into Manchuria at the end of World War II. That's when Marshal Alekasandr Vasilevsky attacked the 2 million men of the Imperial Japanese Army from the east, west, and north in simultaneous blitzkrieg attacks. Under normal circumstances, the attackers would need a 3:1 advantage—6 million men—but Vasilevsky had only 1.6 million under his command. Because of his ability to provide unity of command across all three fronts, he achieved a famous victory in only three weeks, rolling up an area the size of Western Europe.

A typical example of failure to achieve unity of command occurred at Antietam Creek during the American Civil War. General George McClellan failed to unify the command of his sixty thousand Union troops. He lost the opportunity to completely route the numerically inferior Confederate Army of General Robert E. Lee by not ordering an exploitation of extreme Confederate weakness at Piper Farm. Unfortunately for the Union, McClellan didn't have sufficient grip of the forces at his disposal, and an attack on this hole in the Confederate lines didn't materialize. Thus, McClellan lost an opportunity for decisive victory.

ferent leaders have different priorities, and shortages of resources always factor in. As a result, the sales engineers were pulled from pillar to post, and the sales teams never got the undivided commitment they needed.

To further exacerbate matters, the service organization was totally separate and not under control of the sales organization at all. Indeed, each organization had its own sales teams, which had different targets and thus different priorities. Customers came to realize that they'd have to deal with two sets of sales teams—product and service. The real benefit for the customer in buying the company's products was its excellent service and support. Unbelievably, the synergies—sales and service—could never be fully realized because they were sold separately. When you think about deal structuring, you'll see that by separating products and services, the opportunity was lost to put together a package including both elements and then structuring the pricing accordingly.

In terms of engineering and service splitting from the main sales effort, the rationale was more one of dogma than practical necessity.

Over the months, it became increasingly obvious that, unless unity of command was restored, the fragmentation would prevent the teams from acting as a unit to close deals and give customers what they wanted. That, of course, was an end-to-end solution—from presales advice to the implementation of a post-sales customer-care and service program.

The final piece of this dysfunctional mess was the use of "matrix management" to control the resources—a total aberration. Different verticals (financial services, public sector, manufacturing, etc.) had specialist resources located centrally (in London in this case) under the control of directors who carried overlay targets (another pet peeve of mine) that rolled up entire regions (Europe, Middle East, and Africa). In addition, specialist technical resources for various technology groups (data center, software, collaboration, etc.) were organized in a similar way under another set of directors (again based in London).

In addressing concentration of forces, we described the need to mass resources at the *schwerpunkt* (point of focus) to achieve rapid, decisive results. The corollary of that is having the resources themselves under the command of the same person or chaos quickly ensues. So it was in this particular company. Its lack of unity of command made getting the right resources to the right place at the right time difficult. Not only did the directors of the different elements have varying plans and priorities (obviously), but politics and petty rivalries inevitably emerged. They prevented frictionless cooperation that would have been needed to make the matrix system work properly.

Now the reason the company in question attempted this type of model was a problem of coverage. The employees were expected to cover a mass of countries and territories with a limited number of resources. The apparent answer was to centralize specialist resources in London and have the more generic capabilities on the ground. Instead, they attempted to thinly spread across the entire region but deploy key resources where they were most needed. Why is there a problem with this? Because they had no unity of command at a low-enough level (all coming together in terms of command at the VP of EMEA), the entire effort was unfocused and dissipated. Consequently, the resources were never properly concentrated on key areas.

Most militaries have recognized this problem. Any particular army will have infantry, armor, artillery, combat engineer, transport, logistics, and maintenance support within its own organization and command structure. For operational purposes, these resources are split into multifunctional battle groups of around 1,200 men and women with all facets of the army's resources represented. They are grouped under a single battle group commander who has complete unity of command. It is up to the commander to position and utilize the men, women, and material as he or she sees fit to execute the plan. Liaison and matching of plans between peers becomes unnecessary; the battle group commander can carry out the mission unimpeded by anyone else other than the enemy.

In my business example, my recommendation for the company was to make big bets on the key areas where the leaders wanted to focus. (Once again, the goal is concentrating resources where you believe you can achieve a breakthrough in strategic accounts or even in strategic countries.) Having chosen these areas, I recommended putting the right resources under the command of the geography leader and letting him get on with it.

These are the key advantages of this unity of command:

- Resources can be allocated according to one plan—a plan created by the geography leader.

- Priorities are clear to all personnel. In case of a conflict, they will turn to only one person to resolve it.

- Resources can be concentrated in the right areas and accounts to achieve breakthrough.

- Should changes in direction be required, they can be implemented quickly and decisively.

Team Structure

It's essential to get organized for success. For any team that wants to be at a high state of competitive readiness, the structures, lines of reporting, and performance expectations need to be clear and well practiced. But how can you structure the sales teams efficiently? Let me share a classic approach.

Sales Managers

Earlier, we discussed how to achieve focus on accounts by allocating high-touch, strategic account managers/salespeople. They need to be managed by a direct line manager; in most companies I've worked with, that person holds the most critical position in the company. Most frequently referred to as a regional sales manager (RSM), this person will have between six and eight salespeople reporting to him or her and will drive success or failure in any set of accounts.

Key elements of this role include the following:

Strategy—Devolve strategy for the team from the overall company strategy document. This means making the strategy relevant and clear for the salespeople so they can derive their own individual strategies.

Planning—Put together a detailed plan that can act as a foundation for individual plans. From there, provide constant verification of successful execution or deviation from those plans.

Forecasting—Continually drive accurate and aggressive forecasting with a strong emphasis on successful execution. This is the heartbeat of the selling effort, and the regional manager provides the impetus.

Innovation—Continually demand and drive innovative ideas from the salespeople. It's too easy to become a numbers machine with no emphasis on innovation in the accounts.

Motivation—Balance group, task, and individual needs (see chapter 6 on the maintenance of morale) to maintain forward momentum. The secret to the success of any team is the motivation of team members; the regional sales manager is in charge of concocting it.

Customer relationships—Maintain relationships at a high level in the account. While the account managers (AMs) own the customer engagements and have the primary relationship, the regional manager (RM) needs to be involved. Although the RM won't in any way undermine the AM, the RM will provide an escalation point, a level of stability to provide continuity should AMs change. The point is to add value to the relationship.

Problem resolution—As they go about their business, the salespeople will come up against multiple challenges both internally and with the customer. They're at the front line and greatly exposed, risking their livelihoods (no sales, no income) and usually their position with the customer (coming under customer scrutiny to see if exacting requirements are being met). It's often extremely helpful to have an experienced RSM who knows the customer and the company well and who can get issues fixed. (It's tough to come into a new company and be an effective RSM, which is worth noting for future hiring. It's often best to promote the AMs who show the right aptitude rather than bring in RSMs from outside.) The best RSMs I've met are good at many things, but fixing issues is the skill that sets the best ones apart from others.

Provision of focus—Salespeople often talk about their managers protecting them from management in the organization. Or to the contrary, they say their managers leave them to fall prey to an imaginary set of devils in the boardroom —burning up their time, demanding data, increasing targets, forcing diving catches, etc. Largely, I regard this as nonsense. Enterprise and even medium-sized organizations are, by their nature, somewhat chaotic, and thus unexpected requirements crop up. The RSM needs to keep the team focused on the plan and on the daily activities of executing that plan. Everything else must be dealt with in that context.

Momentum assurance—Over and above the forecast, the RSM needs to drive the actions of team members. RSMs should have lists of actions with timelines, responsible personnel, and updated comments that are reviewed at forecast meetings. It's also important for them to encourage AMs to keep similar lists at a more micro level. That ensures they're relentlessly following up on the actions discussed in every one of their meetings.

Sales Directors

Typically, sales directors have three to four regional managers reporting to them and roll up their individual RM targets into one number. The director probably reports to a sales VP along with three other peers. The job of sales director can be tough because it's often difficult to decide exactly what's required. I'm quite clear about this, however. Let's go into this in detail.

Vision and strategy—Typically, a sales director will either be responsible for a specific industry vertical (e.g., oil/gas, manufacturing, etc.) or for a geographical region. Continual increases in complexity of the market sometimes lead to matrix organizations that involve vertical and geographic overlays. As you've seen, I abhor this approach because it severely conflicts with the principle of unity of command. So, as an example, let's assume a straightforward role for the director in a vertical or geographic area. The director will have a clear directive from her VP about the overall vision and strategy for the company, but it will be quite generic. She needs to take this and provide specificity for her area of responsibility. For example, if the corporate strategy is to increase market share in data storage, then a director in oil and gas might derive a strategy to penetrate the real-time process-control data centers of oil refineries and petrochemical plants and the upstream activities of the exploration and production sector. She'll have to research the market and her own teams before making that kind of derivation. However, it's an incredibly important decision because it will drive the effort of thirty or so salespeople and an equivalent number of technical resources for twelve months.

Execution—The numbers from all of the RSMs roll up to the director, who will carefully monitor progress. I've found that RSMs are so busy in the rough and tumble of battle that they often cannot provide strategic guidance.Instead, they're overly focused on deals and probably aren't able to identify when changes of direction, reinforcements, or withdrawal are required. The director, on the other hand, does have the luxury of more time and perspective to do this. That person should be able to intervene early to make sure any underperformance is addressed proactively and new opportunities are properly staffed and exploited.

Business information—To execute well, the director needs to have accurate, extensive, near-real-time information on sales, pipelines, etc. In some organizations, this information is provided in spades, but usually it's surprisingly scant. The director is challenged to find a way of getting, maintaining, and presenting accurate business information to be able to execute. This may take a lot of informal communication with the finance teams rather than a more formal promulgation of data. However, a director who doesn't self-generate a set of spreadsheets will never succeed. It's absolutely no good saying it's someone else's responsibility. Rather fighting for and maintaining this data is the director's job—a key piece of the value the person in this position adds.

Focus—The director is also in a good position to rationalize the stream of requests for data and actions that come down from the top of the organization. This flow of requests can't be rebuffed, but it can be fielded, reshaped, and addressed in a sensible way. There's no value in simply passing requirements down the line using your e-mail's forward function. I would expect directors to seek to understand the reason for every "fire drill" and then minimize the disruption for RSMs and AMs. How? This is done by rationalizing requests, adding as much value as possible, and passing down only items that can't be addressed elsewhere. The most classic example of this is sudden requests for pipeline and forecast data that corporate leaders require for meetings, briefings, manufacturing, etc. In a poorly organized company, these requests drop right to the AMs without any value added from above. Effective directors, though, have all this information (no more than a week old) on their PCs. They can e-mail pertinent data without even opening the file. Often, the AMs never even know about the requests. That signifies real value from a leader!

Customer relationships—With up to three hundred accounts in any particular director's area of responsibility, trying to develop relationships across the entire customer population wouldn't be scalable or sensible. This is when strategic account segmentation can be helpful. I recommend directors focus only on the strategic accounts and then run regular reviews on those and deal with the remainder of the accounts on a rolling basis. This means customer meetings can be limited to the CxO suite of the half-dozen strategic accounts in the director's territory. As a result, those meetings can be highly effective, complete with meaningful follow-up. It bothers me to see meetings generate a series of undertakings and actions only to have follow-up peter out through lack of focus or attention to detail. While this is unacceptable at AM level, at the director level, it's disastrous. When senior sales leaders visit me for advice in my role as a managing director, I'm often astonished to learn how many commitments are broken through poor or nonexistent follow-up. It creates a negative impression of the salesperson as an individual and of the company as a whole.

The lesson? If you promise to do something, make sure you do it. You'd be surprised how many customers take note of how you fulfill your commitments. It's normally a harbinger of what will follow in the account relationship.

Sales Vice President

The sales vice president is ultimately responsible for the vision, strategy, and execution of the team. This person needs to be able to take the vision and strategy of corporate and turn those into a workable plan that can be executed. In addition, the sales VP is required to organize resources into a structure that is ready for action and can adequately deal with the rigors of the market—all while executing corporate strategy.

At this level, an individual could have up to six directors reporting to him or her with approximately 30 RMs and 180 AMs, plus all of the engineering personnel and sales operations teams. Given this daunting responsibility, the sales VP needs staff to ensure proper conduct throughout the operation. The skeleton of this team best looks like this:

- **Chief of staff (or head of sales operations)**—The chief of staff is responsible for the overall plan and its promulgation and execution as it pertains to the directors. This person arranges for and runs regular reviews with the directors and the VP, including weekly forecast calls. Administrative duties— HR reporting issues, commissioning and pay, training, etc.—are part of the chief of staff's responsibilities, freeing the VP to deal with strategic concerns.

- **Financial controller**—The key responsibility for this person is providing business information. In many companies, this information is at a premium, and directors and the people reporting need to compile their own data. This notwithstanding, the financial controller spends the bulk of his or her time ensuring the VP has the necessary information to drive the operation's decision making. The financial controller is also responsible for controlling expenses and setting budgets, targets, and goal sheets in close liaison with the VP.

- **Head of HR**—This position is primarily responsible for the whole HR effort in the operation, with a critical responsibility for recruitment and talent acquisition. Even in a dreaded recruitment freeze, the hiring teams in HR should be researching and interviewing talented candidates to be signed up at the earliest opportunity. The HR team is also responsible for exiting underperforming resources, thus creating an ongoing need for new blood.

Returning to the role of the Senior Vice President (SVP), it's important for that person to stay high level and not get sucked into micromanagement. Over and above the planning function, the SVP's key responsibilities are as follows:

- **Continual monitoring of execution against the plan**— As mentioned previously, no plan survives contact with the market, so the VP is constantly adjusting the plan, ensuring changes are communicated and executed. With ongoing new threats from competitors and from customers themselves, a continual trimming of the sails is required. At the same time, the VP relentlessly drives the sales numbers.

- **Customer relationships**—For the sales VP, customer relationships are exclusively at the strategic account level and mostly with CEOs and CIOs. These relationships should not be perfunctory or courtesy driven but meaningful and complete with follow-ups. The staff and account teams provide the framework of minutes of meetings and actions to allow effective, verifiable follow-up to take place.

- **Communications**—Without question, team leaders need to communicate with their teams. At the VP level, teams tend to be geographically dispersed, possibly globally. This makes it extremely important for the sales VP to consistently project his or her personality, plan, and requirements down to the AM level. However difficult, communicating well must be a priority.

Conclusion

Unity of command is about giving leaders overall responsibility with authority. The idea of matrix management simply does not work. Leaders must be given the autonomy to set priorities, make decisions, and execute their plans without worrying about negotiating with other leaders to concentrate resources at key points in the market. Having a team structure and procedures in place is critical to a successful execution. The AM, RSM, director, and VP hierarchy described here provides the ideal model for success.

8   Economy of Effort

We must not try to use force only in an overwhelming capacity, but in the proper capacity, and in a precise and principled manner.——**Mike Mullen**, *former chairman of the US Joint Chiefs of Staff, 2008*

"Doing more with less" has become today's business mantra. It's not a matter of battening down the hatches to get through the latest recession; in our volatile and unpredictable world, smarter working now has to be "business as usual."——**Jane Simms**, *writer*

Economy of effort is a critical principle of warfare that addresses getting the most out of the resources available to you. It's a culmination of the principles of concentration of force, offensive spirit, and selection and maintenance of objectives. In essence, it means strike with an appropriately sized, aggressively minded sales force that's concentrated on a set of well-chosen objectives.

It's the correct sizing that's important here. In the run-up to the first Gulf War, Chairman of the US Joint Chiefs of Staff Colin Powell—later US secretary of state—developed the Powell Doctrine. This doctrine demanded the use of overwhelming force against an enemy to destroy him at minimum loss of personnel and material. This "sledgehammer to crack a nut" approach has been discredited in recent years because of the large numbers of simultaneous demands on US forces throughout the world. This has made it impossible to deploy the huge amounts of force needed to fulfill the Powell Doctrine. Thus, a "more with less" approach has been adopted. This has involved leveraging IT resources to massively increase intelligence on the enemy. The approach has also employed unmanned airborne vehicles (drones) to gather intelligence and deliver weapons as well as teaming with allied armies and intelligence services and countless new high technology innovations. All of these aim to reduce the need for troops on the ground.

In actuality, resources are always in short supply on the battlefield. All the way down to platoon level, the military has adopted a philosophy that personnel must be permanently focused on the tasks in hand. Therefore, orders need to be clear, and individuals can't be in any doubt of what's required of them. Invariably downtime occurs, so each soldier is encouraged to prepare to execute the missionduring this time.

At higher formation level, this philosophy is extrapolated by ensuring all units are properly engaged to fulfill the mission. Everything and everybody acts as one to fulfill a common purpose. Doing so minimizes waste and leverages available resources as much as possible.

I am extremely interested in the way economy of force—or economy of resources—translates into business. We hear a lot about right-sized firms that have been cut to the bone with not a single ounce of fat left. IT and collaboration technologies have become "force multipliers," enabling leaders to get enhanced levels of productivity out of their teams. And to some extent, that's true.

No one can deny that using extensive business information and productivity software tools, audio-video conferencing, and mobile technology have massively increased individual productivity. However, I would question how fully these improvements are being leveraged. Are they actually getting the most from the teams to deliver maximum effect on the customers' businesses?

I often ask groups of assembled salespeople, "How many of you don't have enough time to do everything that's expected of you?" Needless to say, a forest of hands goes up. There's a lot of peer pressure at work, of course. No one wants to be the employee who's not busy or not pulling his weight. But, by the same token, I rarely speak to salespeople who don't tell me individually that they're too busy to cope with everything expected of them. Frankly, I believe they *think* that's true. But people on both failing and successful teams tell me the same thing.

The point is this: Team members must have their energies directed properly. Given the key principles of selling that we have already discussed, we have a fantastic set of plans and objectives for our sales effort. At this point, the challenge is ensuring all team members—salespeople or presales people, administrators, marketers, and so on—understand the plan and are striving to fulfill it.

This doesn't mean you have to micromanage every person you're responsible for; on the contrary, your role is to communicate the plan and how it's extracted down to individual levels, then let the team get on with it. This seems obvious, but it's much harder to achieve than you'd think. And the difficulty increases with teams dispersed across large areas, many working from home and often in different time zones and continents.

Specifically, the "One Team with a Common Purpose" message must get passed to all of these dispersed people. It's the sales manager who needs to apply the GOYA principle and ensure that everyone is pulling *in the right direction*. That's not micromanagement; it's a vital part of sales leadership.

The following techniques will help you to set up and keep a grip on the team dynamic without individuals feeling they're losing autonomy— a morale killer for a lot of people:

- When communicating the plan, continually make sure team members understand not only their parts of it, but also the bigger picture. For example, you may only be briefing on the Frankfurt part of the effort, but it's interesting for teams to know what's going on in London and Dubai and how it feeds into the greater EMEA effort. People like to have context; it helps them feel they're contributing to a bigger goal.

- Be sure people are clear about their parts of the plan in terms of their SMART objectives and where they're aiming to go. Get them to play back exactly what's required of them to ensure they're thinking about what interactions will be required with their peers and presales colleagues.

- Have individuals mind map their plans for fulfillment of objectives and then capture those plans in a series of actions. Make them own the list of actions and review it with them regularly, ideally at least once a month.

- Visit individuals personally as often as you can, combining your visit with sales calls to see how they're doing with their customers. You can tell a lot about good AMs on this kind of visit. Do they know the security personnel? Do they have a badge for the customer site? Can they find offices quickly? Do they appear to be known around the corridors? Are their customers up-to-date with the messaging?

Conclusion

If you can drive home the common purpose message with these techniques, you're well on the way to delivering an economy of effort or economy of resources. Be careful about carrying dead wood. I find that larger companies have big clusters of vertical (oil, gas, finance, etc.) and horizontal (database, ERP, complimentary applications, etc.) overlay teams. They are full of intelligent, well-meaning people, but from a command structure point of view, they appear to be out of the loop of the main selling effort. Thus, they're a prime example of resources that aren't properly united for a common purpose, and to a large extent, they are wasted.

Also beware of "business development" titles because people in these roles can be running their own agendas, often chasing personal interests and hobby horses that are off message from the plan. They may be nice to talk to, but they're not part of the economy of effort principle because they're not partaking in your common purpose.

9   Maneuver to Win

Battles are won by slaughter and maneuver. The greater the general, the more he contributes in maneuver, the less he demands in slaughter.—**Winston Churchill**, *British prime minister*

I don't look to jump over seven-foot bars: I look around for one-foot bars that I can step over.—**Warren Buffett**, *American investor*

In business, when vying with competitors for customer business, maneuver becomes a crucial principle to keep the opposition continually off balance. The Chinese philosopher Sun Tzu (you knew he'd pop up eventually) counsels us to choose the battlefield and draw the enemy on to it. That means maneuvering the customer's requirements and expectations to suit our strengths, thus putting the opposition at a disadvantage. Your competition will be trying to do the same to you, so you have to be cognizant and react to that.

I'd like to use an example of a battle royal between two companies for a government contract to provide a network for the armed forces. One company was well established with the customer and had developed a nonstandard voice and data network that suited the customer perfectly. It provided the required utility and security and fitted the deployment footprint. It also appeared to meet the pricing and budget profiles specified by the government. Sounds like "game over," doesn't it?

The second company attacked this seemingly impregnable position by introducing a solution that utilized industry standard protocols; it was not specifically developed for the customer. At first, this was of no consequence to the customer, but the sales teams started to spread fear, uncertainty, and doubt by suggesting that a nonstandard solution wouldn't

In battle, the principle of maneuver is used to catch the enemy off balance, to out-flank and defeat him before he can readjust. A contemporary and effective example of maneuver was Major General James Mattis's First Marine Division's charge from Kuwait to Baghdad during Operation Iraqi Freedom in 2003. At the start of the invasion, six Iraqi divisions were positioned along what the Iraqis presumed would be the allies' invasion route, the Tigris River. After initial engagement, however, Mattis diverted the division westward through the area between the Tigris and the Euphrates Rivers. This action totally outmaneuvered the Iraqi army. They ended up only one hundred kilometers from Baghdad where the enemy had managed to po-sition a blocking division. Once again, Mattis maneuvered past the defenders, this time eastward. After an iconic tank charge of more than one hundred kilometers, they ended up on the brink of the city.

It's a good example of how constant change and movement can typically bypass the enemy and achieve strategic objectives without ever engaging a fight.

support changes in industry software and hardware. The customer could be unknowingly left with a white elephant.

This turned out to be an amazing maneuver because it pulled the rug out from under the feet of a firmly entrenched competitor. All of a sudden, the competitor's carefully developed and positioned offering was being questioned by all of its erstwhile proponents in the govern-ment. So successful was this approach that the competing company had to start repositioning an industry standard protocol by making a hurried and ultimately doomed alliance with a partner. Within weeks, the com-petitor's position had been totally undermined.

As ever, technology can play a critical part in the maneuver prin-ciple. In a second example, I cite a competition to supply a multinational enterprise with video-conferencing equipment. The RFP process was being run by procurement. As a result, a great deal of commoditization occurred among the competing companies.

The company I was supporting figured out that about 40 percent of the costs to the customer lay in building the infrastructure, as opposed to 60 percent for end points (the cameras and screens). In an interest-ing and devastating maneuver, the company took the infrastructure into the cloud and then charged the customer a subscription fee to access it as an *operational* cost rather than a *capital* expenditure. Its aim was to amortize the cost of the infrastructure over several customers. By doing this, the company turned the competition on its head in one stunning day. Not only had the company provided a viable technical solution, but this solution allowed the customer to slash 40 percent of its estimated CAPEX costs. After proposing a solution that the customer hadn't even requested, the company was awarded its business.

Conclusion

Maneuver is a great technique for unbalancing your competition by changing the game, choosing new playing fields, and persuading customers to realign to your value proposition. It requires out-of-the-box thinking and courage to turn perceived norms on their heads. When well executed, maneuver can be a devastatingly effective principle of selling.

10 Security

He shall spurn fate, scorn death, and bear His hopes 'bove wisdom, grace and fear:And you all know, securityIs mortals' chiefest enemy.
—**William Shakespeare**, *Macbeth*

In war, security is all about preventing the enemy from surprising you and thereby gaining an unexpected advantage. It's about keeping your strategic and tactical information secure and using intelligence to know as much about your enemy's intentions as possible.

We've discussed surprise and maneuver to defeat our competition in business, and information security is a key issue. It's critical to continually remind teams that they need to be extremely cautious with their information. I'm frequently amazed to see people working on laptops with no screen guard to protect from Peeping Toms. And I often hear salespeople talking at the tops of their voices in bars and airport lounges about what one can only imagine are commercially sensitive topics. This simple type of insecurity is easy to overcome, but you'll find that teams need continual reminders. I recommend the use of secure e-mail services and locked-down laptops to prevent lost machines from being used to gain competitive information. Information security in the office requires a carefully deployed IT infrastructure. Paper notes and printed documents should be shredded as soon as people are finished with them. White boards should be wiped at the end of sessions. I know this advice sounds paranoid, but it's astonishingly easy to find out what your competition is doing by keeping your ear to the ground. Don't fall into the same trap.

On the other side of the coin, it's easy to get a strong feel for your competition's general go-to-market approach from websites and market-

In the buildup to the Battle of Kursk, Germany's plans were compromised months before its attack on the neck of the Kursk salient. As a result, the Red Army was able to build 250 kilometer-deep mine fields, tank traps, anti-tank guns, and artillery kill zones. As a result, when the expected massive German assault came, the Russians were able to hold it up, sap the energy from it, and counterattack with devastating results. This essentially ended the war in the east.

World War II provided another example of security being critical to success. The British broke the Germans' Enigma coding system with the Ultra program, which gave the Allies the ability to decrypt huge numbers of messages—a massive boon to the Allied war effort. It's suggested that Ultra actually shortened the war by up to two years.

ing collateral and, more importantly, from current and former employees. Most industries are relatively cliquey, and having associates and friends in competitive organizations is quite common. In the course of conversations, you can easily build a general picture of what's going on in their companies. In addition, your customers give a lot of clues through the questions they ask you, what they tell you, and how they behave when you ask them specific questions about your approach.

Conclusion

Keeping commercial and strategic information secure is essential to maintaining competitive advantage. Sales leaders must take responsibility for ensuring their teams are continually briefed on the need to maintain security procedures.

Keep in mind that competitors may also be less secure than they should be. An attentive business leader can pick up on useful indications of competitive intent.

11 Flexibility

To ensure attaining an objective, one should have alternate objectives. An attack that converges on one point should threaten, and be able to diverge against another. Only by this flexibility of aim can strategy be attuned to the uncertainty of war.—**Sir Basil H. Liddel-Hart**, *military strategist*

Stay committed to your decisions, but stay flexible in your approach. —**Tom Robbins**, *author*

Sir Basil Liddel-Hart's quotation sums it up for me. No amount of planning ever survives first contact with the enemy. It's guaranteed you'll have to be flexible as soon as you begin fighting—or even before that.

Highly rigid plans simply don't succeed. This was illustrated by the remarkably static approach of the Iraqi Army in both the first and second Gulf Wars. Their military forces were comprehensively outmaneuvered without much reaction on their part. This indicated a lack of initiative on the ground and poor command and control at higher echelons, which should have been able to react quickly to enemy action and changing circumstances.

Before leaving the military examples, let me refer to the thinking of Martin van Creveld, a military strategist. He said that flexible forces are well-rounded and self-contained and have redundancy built into their structures. Adding to these assertions while moving into the context of business and selling, I offer these explanations:

- **Well-rounded** refers to the training and capabilities of individuals on the ground. Well-rounded soldiers have the ability to think on their feet and apply their combat training to adjust actions to suit the unfolding environment. "Adapt—use your head" is the cry. In sales, it's more than this. Yes, we need high levels of initiative, but salespeople have to understand the customer's requirements and constraints and then adapt their approaches accordingly. This means having highly developed skill sets to use as needed. I expect salespeople to have customer industry knowledge, technical capability vis-à-vis their product, operational understanding of their own business processes, and financial understanding and savvy. Beyond that, they need the ability to pull it all together into a package as conditions on the sales battleground change.

- **Self-contained**, in the military, means that from low-level echelon formations upward, units have a high degree of capability under command. At the eight-man section level, for instance, the group will have heavy machine guns and antitank capability, mine-detecting equipment, communications gear to go up two levels of the command structure, alternate commanders, and so on. At battle-group level, there will be a mix of tanks, armored infantry vehicles, combat engineering capability, and artillery, as well as a carefully crafted and totally flexible command-and-control system. Even at the lowest level of the organization, a great deal of flexibility is built into the unit. Local commanders have the resources at their fingertips to take initiative and solve problems as they occur. Clearly, flexibility is designed into the structure. In sales, this is rarely the case, which I find rather worrisome. When I talk to salespeople, one of my biggest gripes is that they seem to rely on other resources to carry out what appear to me to be simple tasks. But you can't always have sales engineers with you. Therefore, it's critical to know a lot of product information that can be applied to the sales discussion. You can't be constantly looking for assistance from vertical and horizontal experts or waiting for a deal specialist to structure financing for you. I accept that teams need access to experts from time to time, but I strongly urge all salespeople to get "tooled up." Do the training, reading, and learning to make yourself a self-contained sales professional. This brings value to your customer and sales success to your company.

- **Redundancy**, a key tactical principle in the military, is the use of reserves to enhance flexibility. Even at platoon level, one section is used as a tactical reserve. At the strategic level, I've mentioned Patton's strategic reserves coming into play at the Battle of the Bulge to relieve the 101st Airborne. In sales, it's not quite that simple. When discussing economy of force, I empha-sized wanting all of our resources driving toward a common purpose at a high tempo. This makes it tough to reconcile having redundancy built into the equation, but we can draw a principle from this. In strong teams I've worked with, when something has to be done for a customer, team members adopt a can-do spirit, and roll up their sleeves, and use the best resources in the team to get it done. Salespeople don't naturally behave like this. I often hear them saying things like, "If it doesn't affect my number, I'm just not doing it." This ugly attitude doesn't get you far if you're in a good team or company. I've seen teams that have used their best financial account managers to structure deals and then in return have given the manager help in an area of weakness—say, contract preparation. So within a sales team, it makes sense to build in redundancy of skill sets and an atmosphere that encour-ages everybody to contribute to the greater good of the whole team.

Saying No Doesn't Indicate Much Flexibility

If there's one thing in selling that drives me completely crazy, it's the use of the word "no" delivered without an incredible amount of care. This subject is contentious because a lot of business people criticize account managers for entirely the opposite reason—that is, they say they don't know how to say no to the customer. For the salesperson, this results in a bewildering dichotomy that many never get corrected.

In tightly controlled corporations—and plenty have emerged after Enron and Worldcom—salespeople often fear for their lives if they deviate even slightly from a stringent set of rules. I understand this, and

Multiple examples of flexibility in warfare exist. Liddel-Hart's idea of having alternative objectives even when planning is best illustrated by General William Sherman's March to the Sea in 1864 during the American Civil War. His plan was to create a line of advance with multiple objectives to keep the Confederate Army guessing his real intentions. In the first instance, he planned to take Macon and Augusta. During the advance, he changed his objectives to Augusta and Savannah, and in the end, he actually captured Savannah.

Another favorite example of strategic flexibility comes from World War II during the Battle of the Bulge in 1944. In this battle, the massive German counterattack aimed at splitting the American and British armies and attacking Antwerp. General George Patton's 101st Airborne Division was enveloped and trapped in the town of Bastogne. However, Patton relieved the division by moving a large percentage of his Third Army 240 kilometers in less than a day. This was possible because Patton had planned for the probability of the German counterattack and had enough flexibility built into his plans to counter the Germans' success at Bastogne.

I applaud the rigorous application of rules to defend the interests of all stakeholders. Still, we have to teach our salespeople to be flexible while working within those rules. As a purchaser, what pushes my button are statements such as, "No, we can't do it that way because our system won't allow it." Like all customers, I don't care about my suppliers' systems; I care about *me* and *my company*. I'm looking for solutions to my need, not a lesson in how vendors run their businesses.

A couple of classic examples follow to show you what I mean about flexibility and using initiative on the ground to get around saying no.

In a sales meeting, a customer needs to purchase a complex system involving product, service, and consultancy and demands pricing tomorrow at the latest. The salesperson has to go through a complicated sign-off process, which realistically can't be done in the requisite timeframe. I understand it doesn't make sense to promise the pricing and then fail to deliver it. I imagine you're thinking this: it's about expectation setting, and the customer needs to know the request is impossible. Again, I can't disagree, but salespeople can find ways of dealing with that request.

From my perspective, if the salesperson said, "No, you'll have to wait" (I know—or hope—it wouldn't be that blunt), then I'd be aggravated and impatient to get the salesperson out of my office so I could call someone else. Instead, the salesperson should be flexible and say, "Well, it's tough to get firm prices for you by tomorrow because of controls that are in place to protect our customers. But if it's acceptable, we could at least get you some budgetary numbers to allow you to ask for funding. Then we can follow up with a firm price on Friday." That might not always work, but it beats saying no by a wide margin.

Another classic example is credit facilities. Customers are often short on cash but long on profit. They have the ability to buy and pay for goods and services only if they can get the credit terms. Again, this issue is contentious; its opens discussions about bad debt, salespeople selling above customers' credit limits, and more.

However, without taking risks, salespeople can help in open further channels of finance. The best account managers can introduce customers to leasing companies, vendor financing options, and banks that may help acquire credit. For big deals, this approach is almost a de facto piece of the negotiations. For a customer short on cash flow, it's difficult to overestimate the positive effect of a salesperson assisting with credit.

Flexibility brings up another favorite topic—deal structuring. Salespeople often get into situations in which price has become the deal breaker. This is never a good position to be in. Why? Because when the only item to discuss is price, it's a win-lose situation. When negotiating, always keep multiple areas and issues open so you stockpile the raw materials needed for a well-structured deal.

By manipulating all the parameters, flexible teams can come up with creative solutions to deliver customer satisfaction and good deals for their companies. Here are a few approaches I've used and seen others use successfully:

- **Offer discount levels based on revenue.** In a typical discussion between sales manager and account manager, the sales manager puts forth these questions: If we give the customer this (high) level of discount, what type of business will we see moving forward? How do we recover from this level back to a more normal discount? Here, I typically suggest the account manager use a target-based discount level and rebate. If customers reach a certain revenue target at one level of discount, then move them to a higher discount and provide a rebate on the first round of revenue to make good up to the level of the new discount. This drives customers to reach spending targets, not only to attain the discount moving forward, but also to achieve a rebate on the spend they'll make entering into the deal. The account manager inevitably needs to encourage flexibility from his finance team in terms of revenue recognition and so on, but this strategy helps overcome objections about price on both sides of the fence.

- **Bring additional products and services to the mix.** When a customer is focused on price for one set of products, you can turn the tide by bringing additional products or services into the discussion. This helps particularly if the additions are higher margin and enable you to create a mixture of goods and services. Ideally, the blended margin is acceptable to your company and allows the customer to feel like he or she is getting a good deal. Indeed, if you do this well, you can bring a whole new set of upsell opportunities to the account. I've seen this work when salespeople introduce services to a negotiation in which the customer didn't initially want any service attachment. Because the sales team associated the services with product discount, however, the customer was given an incentive to take them. Often, that customer became a long-term consumer of those services.

- **Provide credit through leasing.** Apart from the already discussed opening of new credit lines using the contacts and energy of the salesperson, it might be possible to sell operating leases to customers. In these cases, customers never take actual ownership of the goods they're buying but rent the assets from the finance company. This allows them to show the equipment as OPEX and not CAPEX. For many customers, the distinction is important in their budgets. It also gives them an option for a technology refresh after the period of the lease is up. They continue paying quarterly installments, and the technology gets upgraded automatically.

- **Address and fulfill miscellaneous parameters.** Customers often have unusual requirements that salespeople don't necessarily expect but that come to light through strong relationships and good discovery techniques. There may be warranty expectations (e.g., the customer wants the warranty extended or doesn't want it to start until a future time), delivery criteria (e.g., delivery is required within a certain time frame), or various logistics requirements. Nonstandard requests require flexibility from account managers and their companies. Why is it important to find solutions to these needs? First, you'll generate traction having a grateful customer; second, you can more easily negotiate deal closure by adding the customer's parameters to the mix.

Conclusion

Obviously, flexibility is the salesperson's friend. Don't allow your salespeople to say no. Instead, coach them to say things like, "Well, that could be challenging, but let's think about this alternative."

When salespeople empathize with their customers and can offer flexible solutions, they can achieve fantastic results.

12 Perseverance

If you are going through hell, keep going.——**Winston Churchill**, *British prime minister*

The difference between a successful person and others is not a lack of strength, not a lack of knowledge, but rather a lack in will.——**Vince Lombardi Jr.***, American football coach*

Scottish schoolchildren are frequently regaled with the story of Robert the Bruce, one of Scotland's ancient kings, who was resting in a cave after suffering a setback in battle. He was feeling melancholy about his chances of success in the coming fight. Then, it's said, he saw a spider repeatedly struggling to crawl up the wall of the cave despite continual slips backward. Eventually, the spider made it to the top of the cave wall. Robert was inspired to get out and thrash his enemies, spawning this famous maxim: "If at first you don't succeed, try, try, try again."

For salespeople, perseverance is important, but it does need to be tempered by the need to qualify carefully and lose deals early rather than squander resources on a lost cause. (It's worth noting that Hitler's obsession with Stalingrad forced his army into an eventual trap, which could have been avoided by strategic withdrawal.) Notwithstanding the need to qualify carefully, the ability to get on the phone and keep calling despite rejection after rejection is a quality not demonstrated by many people. Still, it's an important part of the sales psyche.

The best salespeople build portfolios of deals. At one end of the continuum, they have secure business that comes with almost no selling effort month after month. Then they have deals that are full of promise and can be relied on to close. Slightly further down the curve, they have pieces of business that need more work and are experiencing active inter-

In warfare, there can be no better example of perseverance and dogged determination than the Red Army's defense of Stalingrad against overwhelming German superiority. My favorite story from this bloody campaign is the terrified plea coming from a command post on the Volga that was surrounded, with the troops' backs to the river and rounds coming through the walls. "What shall we do?" came the request over the radio. "Your duty—stop panicking" came the reply. Despite the odds stacked against them, the brutally cold weather, starvation, and disease, the Russians held the Germans at bay for months and eventually counterattacked, destroying the German Sixth Army.

ference from the competition. These kinds of deals can take months to close and require extreme perseverance. However, these often become the game-changing deals that take their companies into new customers and verticals, providing the beachhead for similar deals moving forward.

Sales leaders need to give their salespeople time to make these deals happen. Imagine how it can be massively demotivating to work on a deal for twelve months, only to be moved off the account before it can close. Not only does this create isolated discontent, but the whole team gets the message that there's no point in embarking on difficult deals because you can't guarantee you'll still be on the account when it hits pay dirt.

Conclusion

The bottom line is that sales leaders have to encourage and embrace perseverance—a critical quality in the sales organization. Team members survive best when they have the ability to take a punch, pick themselves up, dust themselves off, and get straight back into the fight.

One piece of advice remains: Don't let individual salespeople flog a dead horse. Rather, encourage them to qualify ruthlessly and, when warranted, let go of deals as early as possible.

13 Simplicity

To be capable of exhibiting with simplicity the most complicated move-ments of an army—these are the qualifications that should distinguish the officer called to the station of chief of the staff.—**Napoleon Bonaparte,** *French general and politician*

Simplicity is the ultimate sophistication.—**Leonardo da Vinci,** *Italian artist*

Because of the inevitability of things going wrong in battle, the simplest of plans are usually the best. If troops are working to a highly compli-cated set of instructions and then circumstances change through enemy action or unexpected events, chaos can ensue. Simple plans with clean, clear orders are the keys to success.

John Chambers, Cisco's CEO, admitted in 2011 that the company, hitherto famed for its sound strategic approach, had taken missteps by identifying multiple "market adjacencies." These were smart grids, con-nected homes, desktop virtualization, and physical security—well off track from the company's traditional product base. Not only were these alien product verticals, but so many different adjacencies were added that employees became confused. Simplicity was lost and sales and stock price took a consequent hit. The solution, successfully implemented, was to reintroduce a back-to-the-knitting approach and allow the sales teams to get on track.

Conclusion

For salespeople, simplicity is critical. Previous chapters discussed how to construct and promulgate plans and objectives and how sales leaders subsequently need to monitor and adjust them to accommodate changing circumstances. Leaders must identify the critical thrusts of the plan and not sweat the small stuff until the salespeople are making solid progress on the main objectives.

Large corporations have a habit of flooding sales teams with ongoing requirements for data, training programs, market initiatives, and complex sales incentives. While often useful in isolation, they typically distract from the core sales effort. Therefore, sales leaders need to help their teams prioritize and not allow simple plans to become complicated by low-priority clutter. Team members have quite enough issues dealing with their customers without making their tasks more difficult.

A terrible example of overcomplexity, caused by the near impossibility of the task, was the US Army's Operation Eagle Claw in 1980 to rescue the American hostages being held in the US embassy in Tehran. The plan involved a complex set of actions: helicopters and transport planes would land in the Iranian desert (Desert One) from carriers in the Indian Ocean; they would move closer to Tehran to a hide site (Desert Two); then they'd storm the Embassy, having driven into Tehran with the CIA in trucks; and finally they'd evacuate hostages by helicopter from the sports stadium. Tragically, two helicopters of eight didn't make it to Desert One, and another damaged its hydraulics. The spare parts were on one of the aircraft that didn't make it. The commanders decided to abort at that point, but one of the helicopters crashed into a transport plane, resulting in the deaths of eight US servicemen.

14 Legitimacy

There is such a thing as legitimate warfare: war has its laws; there are things which may fairly be done, and things which may not be done.
—**John Henry Newman**, English cardinal

I wouldn't be in a legitimate business for all the money in the world.
—**Gennaro Angiulo**, *New England mob boss*

In a post-Enron world, conducting business legitimately is just as important as similar conduct is in warfare. Stakeholders in any business want to avoid the nasty surprises that illegitimate behavior incurs. Dozens of examples illustrate how a lack of discipline on the part of employees has affected major businesses badly.

Unfortunately, salespeople are particularly vulnerable to bad behavior. They're on the front line of any business, talking to customers with high expectations and often unreasonable demands. At the same time, they're experiencing withering pressure to meet targets from their own managements. As a result, they may be tempted into making mistakes and even doing something illegitimate. Typical examples follow.

- A salesperson may write a "side letter," which is an unauthorized promise to do something when an order is placed. This usually happens because salespeople believe that, once the order is in, they'll be able to persuade their employers to give extra discounts, supply free equipment, or extend warranties. They assume that getting the promise authorized before the order is placed will be too difficult.

Cardinal Newman makes it clear: there is legitimacy in war. At a tactical level, civilians, medical personnel, and prisoners of war have to be protected. Wounded combatants from either side must be treated, and torturing of prisoners is strictly forbidden. Breaking these rules undermines the overall legitimacy of the war effort. One has only to look at the drastic consequences of the Abu Ghraib prison abuses during the 2003 US campaign in Iraq to realize the importance of sticking to the rules of legitimacy.

At a strategic level, the UN recognizes wars as being legitimate only when they're fought in self-defense or for the collective enforcement of the UN Charter. The allied invasion of Iraq in 2003 was illegal from a Charter point of view and did not receive Security Council backing. The resulting protracted carnage of invasion and subsequent insurgency was made all the worse because of ongoing international outrage at the illegitimate nature of the war. As a result, President George W. Bush's reputation has been flawed and his legacy tarnished.

- Salespeople sometimes book soft orders from a reseller or distributor who doesn't yet have an order for the end-user customer. A variation on this theme is channel stuffing, in which revenues are falsely boosted by filling up the resellers' and distributors' warehouses with stock far in excess of what the market demands. The net result in both cases is that revenue is overstated.

- Salespeople may simply take a customer's order with nonstandard discounts or terms and conditions and then endeavor to force it through the company's system. They may argue that it's the end of the period and the company is desperate for business at any cost.

Such illegitimate activity happens when you have highly motivated and deeply pressurized individuals whose refuse-to-lose approach to life *generally* stands you in good stead. At times, though, sales leaders have to help save these people from themselves. Needing a clear set of guidelines, they look to their sales leaders to create an atmosphere that enables them to say to their managers, "Look, we can book this order next week, but it's going to take some unconventional activity to get it done. What do you think?" Of course, the answer should be no. Subsequently, the sales leader needs to adopt a sensible approach to what happens regarding how the forecast is changed. Missing a commit is a lot better than doing something outside of company procedures. Thus, it's much better to admit that your team failed to bring in the order in time and live to fight another day.

In addition, sales leaders are wise to strike a balance between pressuring people to deliver and backing off when it's obvious that everything possible has been done to succeed. Perhaps they conclude it simply won't happen as planned this time around.

Conclusion

Legitimacy has to underpin all your efforts with your sales teams. It's essential that you check strident sales behavior with a strong sense of what's right and wrong. Temper the determination to "make a number" with common sense and an understanding of business rules and legal requirements.

Be sure to train and continually remind your salespeople about their obligations. Also, be firm and fair in applying rules to achieve ongoing legitimacy.

15 Call to Action

An army of lions commanded by a deer will never be an army of lions. —
Napoleon Bonaparte, *French general and politician*

Your role as a leader of salespeople is of the utmost importance. If you do a bad job, the team can never be successful. However, if you execute your role well, you'll have the tremendous satisfaction of heading a team that achieves everything you ask of it and more.

From a professional perspective, there's no better position than to be the leader of a relentlessly triumphant selling machine.

Planning for Sales

Having a clear vision of both the markets you want to address and the products and services you want to sell is critically important. Your strategy provides a design for the sales effort, while your execution overlay gives your salespeople the nuts and bolts of what they need to do in the field to realize your plans. The key planning concepts of centers of gravity and decisive points not only define your critical areas of competitive advantage but also identify where you need to attack your competition.

The supreme importance of an excellent forecast and pipeline combined with the power of weekly commit calls will greatly enhance the performance of sales teams. I urge you as a sales leader to focus on these areas as a matter of utmost importance.

Selection and Maintenance of Objectives

Using well-written, tabulated SMART objectives gives everyone in your organization clear imperatives. Then they know what's expected and how they're performing against matrices. Individuals are incentivized to perform as required while you monitor progress and make the necessary course changes to stay on target. Your focus and continual performance monitoring throughout the period is critical to maintaining all of the objectives.

Offensive Action

Getting your salespeople off on the right foot with a refuse-to-lose attitude—the offensive spirit that makes for a successful team—starts with you. I advise you to maintain a positive attitude and strive to find solutions to every obstacle thrown in your way. Your team will react in kind, and sales will grow as a result. Allow no letup; offensive action needs to be the lifeblood of your team.

Concentration of Resources

To sell successfully into big accounts, adopt the high-touch approach. Big sales can only happen if you focus resources on carefully selected targets and don't allow your sales teams to be spread so thin that they'll inevitably underperform.

Look to select and nurture strategic accounts, and structure your teams to focus on them. Work out how to provide requisite coverage of nonstrategic accounts, ensuring that you build an efficient model that maximizes potential sales from the entire account base.

High Competitive Readiness

You are responsible for the readiness of your teams. They need to have the right types and quantities of product data and customer positioning material to help them be successful. That requires you to ensure not only that they have access to the material but also that they learn it, understand it, and can articulate it. Their job is to provide customers at all levels of an organization with a tailored set of benefits that enunciate your value propositions in a highly compelling manner.

Motivating your teams is critical to competitive readiness. Motivation is driven by a mix of pay plans, recognition, team building, and leadership. Raising the motivation of your teams to the highest level possible is a major factor in their eventual successes.

Leadership and Maintenance of Morale

Through your strong leadership, you can keep your teams succeeding. Focus on the needs of the tasks to ensure completion of your plans. Focus on the teams to drive morale and offensive spirit. And focus on the individuals to maximize motivation. This task is never easy, but such intense focus is necessary to build and maintain high morale.

Unity of Command

Avoid matrix management structures, and put people in sole charge of capable teams. Give them their SMART objectives in the context of your vision, strategy, and execution overlay—then let them get on with it. People always react well to the enhanced responsibility and clarity that a unity of command structure brings.

Economy of Effort

Doing more with less is something you're familiar with, but remember this: inculcating everyone you're responsible for with a common purpose and a desire to succeed will act as a dramatic force multiplier.

Final Points of Action

Make sure that simplicity, maneuverability, and flexibility are watchwords in your approach. You may have to move goal posts and go back on decisions as market circumstances change while you endeavor to trip up your competition. Overly complex plans will make this difficult, and any rigidity of mindset will hamper you. Embrace a highly fluid and flexible approach.

And finally, don't allow all your efforts to be undermined by poor information security or illegitimate behavior by your sales teams. It's heartbreaking to see hard work diluted by avoidable lack of discipline.

There's no better job in the world than leading a sales team. By applying the principles discussed in this book, you will not only enhance your own performance and that of your teams but glean tremendous business success and have fun in the bargain.

Good luck. To the victor go the spoils!

Acknowledgments

I would like to thank all of my family and friends who have supported me as I put this book together, especially Elaine, Suzanna, Grant, and Craig. Thanks for all your understanding, team. I'd also like to thank Rami Musallam of Thrupoint for his critical appraisal of the text. Finally, a big thank you goes to my editor Barbara McNichol, who has given me first-class support in polishing my rough prose and to the marvelous team at Wheatmark—Atilla Vekony, Grael Norton and Kat Gautreaux.

About the Author

Dale Millar served in the British Army for ten years and saw service in the first Gulf War. Latterly, he has worked in the high-tech sales environment in Silicon Valley, the UK, Germany, France, Russia, and the Middle East. He lives with his wife and three children in southwest London, earning a living from his writing and running sales enablement and big data businesses.

Lightning Source UK Ltd.
Milton Keynes UK
UKOW04f1851160215

246387UK00001B/78/P